What's Been Damming Up the Stream?

by
Louis G. Nelson

To Alvin + Bev

Louis

authorHOUSE™

1663 LIBERTY DRIVE, SUITE 200
BLOOMINGTON, INDIANA 47403
(800) 839-8640
WWW.AUTHORHOUSE.COM

© 2005 Louis G. Nelson. All Rights Reserved.

No part of this book may be reproduced, stored in a retrieval system, or transmitted by any means without the written permission of the author.

First published by AuthorHouse 02/04/05

ISBN: 1-4208-1701-9 (sc)

Library of Congress Control Number: 2004099705

Printed in the United States of America
Bloomington, Indiana

This book is printed on acid-free paper.

Unless otherwise indicated, the scripture quotations in this book are from the Good News Bible – (the Bible in Today's English Version) © American Bible Society, 1976

PREFACE

This book was written for folks like me, who have felt some time in their lives, that something has been damming up the stream. Jesus said that there would be *streams of living water* gushing forth from us when we are filled with His Spirit.

But when there is only a trickle instead, we wonder why. Then we look to the Bible to discover what is standing in the way.

This all came into focus for me several years prior to writing this book, when I participated in a spiritual development retreat. Following that retreat the participants formed covenant groups that met monthly for prayer and support.

The covenant binding each group together included such agreements as spending an hour each day in Bible reading, meditation and prayer – praying for each other – and keeping a daily journal.

After several years in such a group, and many years since the group disbanded because of some members moving, I have continued the daily meditation time and keeping a journal. My journal entries have involved scriptural reflection in the form of poetry. Friends who have read some of the poems have encouraged me to share them with a wider audience. My prayer is that they will give some insights in how to remove the debris that is damming up the stream.

Louis G. Nelson

ACKNOWLEDGMENTS

My sincere appreciation and gratitude to two persons close to me, without whose help and participation this book would not be have been ready for publication.

Thank you to my wife, June, and my son Andrew, both of whom who spent many hours proof-reading to discover the many errors in the manuscript I gave them,

And thank you to Andrew for taking the pictures that appear on the front and back covers of this book.

CONTENTS

PREFACE	v
My Greatest Challenge	1
What's Been Damming Up The Stream	3
God Gives Back To Me	5
I Show That I Am God's Servant	7
Silver and Gold	9
Receiving and Giving	11
Hope	13
So What If The Wicked Prosper	15
The People Of God	17
Two Went Up To Pray	19
I Will Send You	21
Answered Prayer	23
Life Style	25
God's Love For Me	27
When Jesus Became Sin	29
I Cannot Really Give To God	31
Praise, Proclaim, and Meditate	33
How Can I Give To The Lord?	35
Amazed!!	37
Success	39
He Didn't Even Ask	41
The Secret	43
FaiTH In The Future	45
A Loser's Faith	47

What God Does Not Do	49
Filling My Every Need	51
Abiding	53
God's Primary Mission	55
God Added Day By Day	57
Not In Chains	59
Abundant Grace	61
Related By Obedience	63
Fill Me With Your Will	65
That They May Be One	67
My Father Sees	69
Ananias and Saphira Today	71
Barnabas	73
Two - Way Faith	75
Open To The New	77
The Lord's Endurance	79
God's Chosen People Today	81
In That Philippian Jail	83
To Be Great	85
The Macedonian Call	87
That Your Love Will Keep On Growing	89
A Great American Heresy	91
Keep On Imitating Me	93
Faith, Hope, and Love	95
Speaking As God Wants Me To	97
Jesus' Return	99
Encouragement!	101

Giving and Receiving	103
The Wonder of God's Grace	105
Paul's Prayer and Mine	107
Do I Still Measure Up?	109
Faith Alone Is Not Enough	111
The War Within Me	113
Time	115
A Light To The Nations	117
What About Me?	119
Faith and God's Word	121
Testing and Temptations	123
God's Powerful Love	125
Love, Faith, and Hope	127
Do You Love Me?	129
Blessed, To Be a Blessing	131
The Importance of Obedience	133
The Whole Armor of God	135
Intercession	137
Free At Last!	139
God's Integrity Test	141
My Stewardship of Words	143

MY GREATEST CHALLENGE

Even though I said, "YES", to the Lord,
I know there are days it won't show
In choices and decisions I make –
My spiritual growth has been slow.

Sometimes my prayers don't get off the ground
And I ask, "Does God hear me at all?"
By now I should be stronger than this;
My spiritual growth's at a crawl.

What has hindered a long steady growth,
So my spiritual life would be strong?
The pages that follow in this book
Might tell me what may have gone wrong.

I really know down deep in my heart
There's a truth I'm reluctant to see –
The one main reason I have not grown
Is not anything else, but me.

WHAT'S BEEN DAMMING UP THE STREAM ?

Jesus often used very graphic and descriptive similes and comparisons to get His message across. At one of the annual festivals He spoke to the people about the vitality of the Holy Spirit, and what it is like when He lives in our hearts, and bubbles over. He compared it with gushing springs of life-giving water.

"Whoever is thirsty should come to me and drink, ...Whoever believes in me, streams of life-giving water will pour out from his heart." (John 7:37-38) The next statement clearly interprets this as a reference to the Holy Spirit, who would come to live in the individual believer.

If such an abundant overflow of power and divine presence is to be the evidence of the Spirit's presence, why is it that we often have but a trickle?

Why be content with a few drops when it's God's will that there be a gushing stream? Who (or what) has been damming up the stream?

WHAT'S BEEN DAMMING UP THE STREAM

All I see is little drops
Coming from within;
Jesus spoke of mighty streams,
Power genuine.

"If you thirst," He said to them,
"Come to me and drink."
Between such power then, and me
Jesus is the link!

Show me what is damming up
The flow from deep in me,
Let Your Spirit now gush forth,
From every barrier, free.

Help me to open up to You
So nothing now be hid;
All hindrance to Your power, Lord,
I wish now to be rid

Prayer: Lord, something is damming up that stream in my heart. Please show me what it is, and give me the courage and ability to remove it.

GOD GIVES BACK TO ME

In Luke 6 there is a principle that most people ignore these days. Verse 38 states it: *"The measure you use for others is the one that God will use for you."*

This is a summary statement of what precedes it. It indicates that God will treat us exactly as we treat other people. It is true in at least these four areas of living:

Passing judgement

Condemning

Forgiving

Giving

In fact, the first part of verse 38 indicates that I will receive a greater and more generous portion from God of whatever it is that I give to others. If I give judgment and condemnation to others, God will give me a more generous portion of judgement and condemnation.

If I give forgiveness to others. God will give me a more generous portion of forgiveness,

It is certainly true that we reap whatever we sow.

GOD GIVES BACK TO ME

Whate'er I give to others
Then God will give to me;
This is a truth of scripture
That I've been slow to see.

If my heart's filled with judgement,
And others I condemn,
That's what God will heap on me,
I dare not blast at "them".

But if I show forgiveness,
And pardon freely give,
God will free me from my sins,
Abundantly I'll live.

Everything that I will sow,
Is just what I will reap;
God will give right back to me,
And in a great big heap.

I'd better then be careful
Of what I give to you,
All that I have given away,
Is just what I'll accrue.

Prayer: *Lord, why have I been so slow to see this? Search me, O God and reveal to me what You see. What have I been giving to others? Help me to sow generously and carefully.*

I SHOW THAT I AM GOD'S SERVANT

There is a basic principle of Christian witnessing expressed in 2 Corinthians 6:4. Many have either forgotten it, never understood it, or have consciously rejected it.

"We show that we are God's servants by patiently enduring troubles, hardships, and difficulties."

How do we handle trouble, hardships and difficulty? Is it by complaining, griping and murmuring – or even demanding our rights? Do we lash back at those we think have caused such trouble?

Is the desire for revenge and getting even our uppermost thought when we have been offended?

Perhaps the major point of our praying should be that the Lord give us strength to abandon our complaining and demanding – and that in their place, that God give us patient endurance. Such patient en-durance then becomes the badge of our being God's servants.

I SHOW THAT I AM GOD'S SERVANT

How do I show I'm a servant of God?
Not by school or degree,
It's not by wielding "an almighty rod"
Or that the future, I see.

I show I am God's by what I endure,
And by the patience I show;
By this I reveal if I am mature,
Or if my growth has been slow.

It's all that I do, and how I do it
That shows whose servant I am;
Meeting trouble and going through it,
And what I do in a jam.

Patient endurance that comes from the Lord;
Reveals that Jesus I serve;
There's no other sign that need be explored,
When this one we can observe.

Prayer: *Lord, teach me the much-needed lesson – that it is not my orthodoxy or creed that identifies me as Your servant, but it is the way I behave. Give me the patient endurance that will point others to You.*

SILVER AND GOLD

Have you ever wondered what would have happened to the lame man at the Temple gate if Peter had had some money in his purse that day? Would he have just given a few coins and then have gone on his way, leaving the man as lame and helpless as before?

If Peter had some money to give he might have depended on it to meet the man's need. He would not have relied on God's greater power to meet an even greater need.

Is it when we are without resources of our own that God's power can best be revealed? Could our prosperity get in the way of God's power to perform miracles?

Perhaps the churches' wealth today has diverted us from depending on the miracle-working power of our God. Could our financial blessing really be a curse?

What a shame that we can no longer say as Peter did in Acts 3:6 – *"I have no money at all, but I give you what I have. In the name of Jesus Christ of Nazareth, I order you to get up and walk."*

SILVER AND GOLD

Peter had no silver or gold
To give as alms that day,
He looked right at the man and told
Him – "Get up without delay."

What would have happened if that day
He'd had some alms to give?
Would he have tossed a coin his way,
And let the beggar live?

"Just let him live in misery,
Toss him a coin or two;
He's really no concern to me,
What more now can I do?"

Such is our present attitude,
We'll give a coin or two,
And maybe speak a platitude,
But not much more we'll do.

Perhaps our trouble now is this:
We've money in our purse.
So we, the power of God dismiss,
Our wealth can be a curse.

Prayer: *Lord, help me to assess accurately my dependence on possessions. Do I rely on them more than on You? Has my wealth hindered the moving power of Your Spirit?*

RECEIVING AND GIVING

The apostle Paul shares a promise in 2 Corinthians 9:11 that most of us have missed: *"He will always make you rich enough to be generous."* This is in a paragraph about people who are urged to give bountifully, and to share freely to help with the needs of others.

The truth is that God will always make me rich enough to be generous, but the degree of my generosity is still up to me. Although I always have enough money to be generous, I am not always willing.

When I am generous, then I receive more. It is then that God gives me more than I need so that I'll always have enough for my needs, and more than enough to give away.

Why is this principle so hard for us to accept these days, and so hard to put into practice? So few among us today are generous in giving to the Lord's work, or in meeting the needs of others.

So few churches have caught on to this blessing as well.

RECEIVING AND GIVING

God has promised that I'll have
Enough to give away;
He'll see that I will have enough
To give from day to day.

But what I give is up to me,
The option still is mine;
I have the choice to freely give,
Or also to decline.

And then, what happens after that
Depends on how I plant;
For stingy giving will result
In living that is scant.

If I'm generous with what I have,
And freely give away,
The Lord will see that I receive
Abundance every day.

It's up to me what I will be,
If rich – or very poor,
The more I give for others' needs,
The more I'll have for sure.

Prayer: *Lord, help me to learn this lesson of generosity. Remind me today that generous planting means generous reaping. I thank You that You have made me rich enough to be generous.*

HOPE

Hope was important to the apostle Paul. One of the places where he writes of it is in Romans 15. *"Everything written in the scriptures was written to teach us, in order that we might have hope."* (verse 4) He writes of it further in verse 13: *"May God, the source of hope fill you with all joy and peace by means of your faith in him so your hope may continually grow."*

Usually we associate Paul with an emphasis on faith or love, but here he lifts up hope as a major goal for the believer. Hope is actually an expression of faith – an assurance and positive expression of our confidence in God regarding the future. It carries overtones of confidence and assurance, and not of doubt or pessimism.

God's gifts of joy and peace, mixed with our faith in Him all work to be there to make our hope abound. Hope helps me know that the future is great. It enables me to endure temporary reverses because it gives me a longer perspective on life. It focuses my mind on the power of God and on the God of power

HOPE

When I get discouraged
And tempted to mope –

When problems surround me
Of magnified scope –

When purpose has left me,
I aimlessly grope –

When despair overwhelms me
At the end of my rope –

When enemies beat me,
And I cannot cope –

When facing destruction
On slippery slope –

'Tis then God surrounds me,
And fills me with HOPE !

Prayer: *Lord, I thank You for faith and love – but today I especially thank You for hope. Help me today to seek ways of expressing and sharing my hope in You. Fill me with joy and peace today so my hope will continue to grow.*

SO WHAT IF THE WICKED PROSPER?

As an old man, David had seen a lot of life. He knew how unfair and unequal life could be. He had observed that the wicked often prosper while the righteous suffer.

In Psalm 37 he tries to set the record straight by reminding his people of a few great truths: *"... the wicked will disappear."* (verse 10) *"The Lord takes away the strength of the wicked."* (verse 17) *"Sinners are completely destroyed and their descendants are wiped out."* (verse 38)

But a key statement of this Psalm is verse 8: *"Don't give in to worry or anger, it only leads to trouble."* How often we express worry or anger over the issue of the wicked prospering while we are in need !

Such a response merely betrays our selfishness, covetousness, greed, short-sightedness, and lack of trust. Whenever I allow worry and anger to control my thoughts and judgements, I become unable to see or think straight, and I begin to wallow in self-pity.

So what if the wicked prosper? The Lord has not closed the books yet.

SO WHAT IF THE WICKED PROSPER

So what if the wicked do better than I?
Does that mean that I am in need?
If so much stuff they're able to buy,
In finances they seem to succeed.

Does that mean that I ought to worry or fret,
Or even that I should get mad,
If they're so prosperous and I am in debt,
And I feel that I have been had?

What good would my worry or anger do me?
Would such action bring me more stuff?
Would anger or worry e'er help me to see
At what point I would have enough?

NO – anger and worry would just tear me down,
No good comes from either at all
With them in my heart, in self-pity I'd drown,
And on God I would not think to call.

Lord, help me to get the right view of this life,
To put all my trust just in You;
Don't let me get caught in that internal strife,
Your values, I want to pursue.

Prayer: *Lord, let me see life from the proper perspective. Let me see the true value of life as You see it. Help me to express gratitude for what I have, and not worry over what I don't.*

THE PEOPLE OF GOD

Paul writes to the Colossians in 3:12 – *"You are the people of God."* In the paragraph that follows he lists some of the conditions that will prevail when we truly are God's people. Those conditions are summed up with the thoughts that surround the three-fold use of the word **must**.

a) *"We **must** clothe ourselves with compassion, kindness, humility, gentleness and patience."* (verse 12) He goes on to add tolerance to the list as well. To be God's people means that we are like God in our life-style.

b) *"You **must** forgive one another just as the Lord has forgiven you."* (verse 13) It must grieve the Lord when we willingly receive forgiveness, but refuse to give it to others.

c) *"Christ's message in all its fullness **must** live in your hearts."* (verse 16) We have so glibly stated that we are God's people, without really thinking what it means. To be God's people means we are like God. It means that we live by God's standards and principles, and that we take on godly attributes.

Why do so few Christians today show any resemblance to Christ?

THE PEOPLE OF GOD

We say that we are God's own folk,
That we belong to Him;
But often that is just a joke,
Resemblance is quite dim.

To be God's people would involve
A life-style just like His,
All that we do would then revolve
About all who God is.

We'd clothe ourselves with God's own traits,
We'd live by God's command;
We'd discard sins and all their weights,
Be known by God's own brand.

As God forgave, then so would we,
We'd never withhold love;
We'd live a life so all could see
That we are God's, above.

Prayer: *Lord, let me be one person today who will be clothed with Your characteristics, who will live a life of forgiveness. May the message of Christ in all its fullness live in my heart today.*

TWO WENT UP TO PRAY

We often compare ourselves with people who are far worse than we are because it makes us feel so good. Jesus knew that this was a strong temptation; so, in Luke 18:9-14 he told the story of the two men who went to the place of prayer at the same time.

One of them, a Pharisee, compared himself to all whom he considered inferior. In verse 11 he prayed: *"I thank you, God, that I am not greedy, dishonest, or an adulterer, like everybody else. I thank you that I am not like that tax collector over there."*

But the other man compared himself with God, and, in verse 13, simply prayed: *"God, have pity on me, a sinner."* Each man received just what he asked for. The tax collector received forgiveness. The Pharisee received nothing since he asked for nothing.

What do we seek when we pray? Is it confirmation that we are so good and righteous, and better than anyone else? Or is it a forgiving, cleansing that comes through repentance? Jesus said two men went up to pray, but only one went back down justified.

TWO WENT UP TO PRAY

Those two who went to church to pray,
Each had important words to say;
And each compared himself that day
To someone else along life's way.

The Pharisee erectly stood,
And said: "O Lord, I sure am good,
I always do the things I should,
I'm best in all the neighborhood."

The tax collector bowed his head,
And very reverently, he said:
"Be merciful, or else I'm dead."
Thus from a life of sin he fled.

God gave to each man what he sought,
The Pharisee had asked for naught;
The tax collector was distraught,
As to his prayer, repentance brought.

This story teaches me of prayer,
And of some things to be aware;
To others – I must not compare,
And sin, to God, I must declare.

Prayer: *Lord, be merciful to me, a sinner. Deliver me from the self-righteous bragging of the Pharisee.*

I WILL SEND YOU

On trial for his life, Stephen faced the very serious charge of blasphemy. His defense statement in Acts 7 is a stirring one indeed. Since his only defense was to establish that Jesus was really the Messiah, his speech was a summary of Israel's history.

In it, he described the encounter between Moses and the Spirit of the Lord by the bush that burned but did not burn up. It was God's call to Moses to be the nation's deliverer from Egyptian slavery. Verse 34 contains great insight into how God worked. It was expressed in four stages:

"I have seen the cruel sufferings of my people."

"I have heard their groans."

"I have come down to set them free."

"Come now, I will send you to Egypt."

Is this the way God intervenes to help and save? YES! The Lord sends someone, and if that someone is not willing to go, the people are not helped or rescued. How critically important then, our obedience becomes!

I WILL SEND YOU

How does God send help these days
To those who suffer and groan?
Are there many different ways
By which God's care is shown?

He looks to see the suffering,
And all our groans He hears;
Salvation, He comes down to bring
Amid His people's tears.

How does such help come down to me?
Just what all does God do?
Not only does he hear and see,
But also He sends you.

And of our need He is aware,
Our suffering does He see;
At times when you are in despair,
'Tis then, that He sends me.

Prayer: *Lord, someone near me today needs help, and has called on You for deliverance. Help me to be alert to such need, and to Your voice as You call on me to help. I want to obey You today.*

ANSWERED PRAYER

Throughout all of scripture there is a strong emphasis on our relationship with other people. It's not that people are more important than God, but the best way to express a relationship with God is to relate properly to people.

Hebrews 10:24-25 gives us three simple statements that help us to relate properly to other believers, and thus, to God. *"Let us be concerned for others"* (verse 24) *"Let us continue meeting together."* (verse 25) *"Let us encourage one another." (verse 25)*

Part of this principle is that the usual way God answers prayer is through people. He meets my need by sending someone to me. This is the way God has always done it. Just as Moses was God's answer to Israel's prayer, so the Good Samaritan was the answer to the prayer of the robbers' victim.

Instead of intervening by some spectacular, supernatural miracle, God usually answers prayer through other people, who are alert enough to the Spirit to obey.

The Lord is looking for such people today, to be the answers to others' prayers.

ANSWERED PRAYER

The more I read in God's own word
The more I learn of prayer,
And my imagination's stirred
By all that I read there.
How often does God intervene
In some direct, strong way?
Most often God will change the scene
Through someone's feet of clay.

For God depends on you and me
To answer prayer today;
And when to Heaven I send my plea,
God may send you my way.
So, as I now begin this day,
I let my Savior know
That willingly to Him I say,
"Where e'er You lead, I'll go."

Someone today is in great need,
Is seeking help through prayer,
He never ever might be freed
Unless with him I share,
If I refuse now to obey
What God tells me to do,
There'll be some prayer out there today
To go unanswered too.

Prayer: *Lord, make me willing to be the answer to someone's prayer today.*

LIFE STYLE

The life style we choose is one of our most important decisions. Paul realized that, and in Ephesians 4:1, gave some advice concerning it: *"I urge you ... live a life style that measures up to the standard God set when he called you."* Then in the sentences that follow he gave them some examples of such a life style.

> *"Be humble"   "Be Gentle"   "Be Patient"*
>
> *"Show your love by being tolerant with one another."*
>
> *"Do your best to preserve the unity which the spirit gives by means of the peace that binds you together."*

How tragic that so many who call themselves Christian today, and so many churches that are "New Testament" churches are so rarely humble, gentle, patient, tolerant, or interested in preserving unity.

Perhaps the greatest perversion in Christianity today is the emphasis on doctrinal and verbal purity, while neglecting the purity of life-style. One who loudly proclaims a close connection to God while living a life opposite to humility, gentleness, patience, tolerance and unity, is just plain hypocritical and not Christ-like.

LIFE STYLE

Churches today are full of folk
Who make the Christian life a joke;
They loudly say that they believe,
But by their lives, our God they grieve.

To think that faith is mostly word,
Is really very much absurd;
Some think what matters most is creed,
For "orthodox" belief, they plead.

But more important than all this,
Than this or that hypothesis,
Than right or wrong words that we say,
Is how we live our faith each day.

What matters most with God, I see,
Is gentleness and unity,
Then tolerance, humility,
And if the Lord is seen in me.

Prayer: *Lord, lead me into a life style that pleases You. Help me today to show humility, gentleness, patience and tolerance. May my life contribute to the unity of Your church.*

GOD'S LOVE FOR ME

Some of the most significant statements about God's love for me are found in Romans 8. The paragraph of verses 31 through 39 begin with four significant rhetorical questions:

"If God is for us, who can be against us?"
(No one of any consequence)

"Who will accuse God's chosen people?"
(Certainly not God!)

"Who then, will condemn us?"
(Not Christ – He pleads **for** us)

"Who can separate us from God's love?"
(No one, and no power)

Then, at the close of the paragraph we are assured that nothing in all the universe is strong enough to separate us from God's love. Nor can we do one thing to stop God from loving us. Neither can we do anything to make God's love for us increase.

Since we humans do not love in that way, it is difficult for us to comprehend it. We withhold love and manipulate with it. We distort it and sometimes destroy it. But God's love for us is constant and eternal.

GOD'S LOVE FOR ME

There's nothing stronger than God's love,
That He extends each day to me,
No force down here – or up above,
Can separate that love from me.

No force that Satan could control,
Can take away that love from me;
God's love is so complete and whole,
That it will always reach to me.

This also means that I can't do
One thing to stop that love for me;
No sin that I might e'er pursue,
Could kill the love God has for me.

This is such an awesome fact,
That God will keep on loving me;
There's not one thing – to be exact,
That e'er can take such love from me.

Prayer: *Lord, I cannot fully comprehend Your love, but I feel it. I know that it is there. Enable me to reflect it to others today.*

WHEN JESUS BECAME SIN

One of the great mysteries of the gospel is expressed in 2 Corinthians 5:21 – *"Christ was without sin, but for our sakes God made him share our sin in order that in union with him we might share the righteousness of God."* It is almost impossible for us to comprehend how the sinless Son of God could share our sin.

There are, in fact, several aspects of this that are hard to understand.

What was it like for Jesus to be without sin? Were temptations real? Could He have sinned?

Think how repulsive it must have been for Him, a holy God, to take our sin on Himself.

The text says: *"God made Him to share our sin."* Was Jesus forced to do this, or was it a willing, voluntary act?

Did Jesus feel contaminated and degraded by this whole process? Was He eager to get back to a sinless environment after completing His mission?

Though I don't understand it at all, I do praise God that Jesus made it possible for me to share the righteousness of God.

WHEN JESUS BECAME SIN

I wonder how my Savior felt
When down to earth, He came,
When here amid our sin He dwelt,
Did He feel any shame?

It's clear that He was without sin,
What did that do to Him?
Did He back off – rebel within?
At prospects just too grim?

I think He willingly came down,
Became a human man,
Gave up His power and His crown,
The gulf of sin to span

And now, God's righteousness is mine,
His goodness, I can share;
All this is by my Lord's design,
Revealing His great care!

Prayer   *Lord, how wonderful it is that I need not understand everything in order to experience Your blessings! Thank You for exchanging my sin for Your righteousness.*

I CANNOT REALLY GIVE TO GOD

Although God did not allow David to build the Temple, he was allowed to gather much of the material that Solomon would use for its construction. 1 Chronicles 29:10-14 records David's prayer of dedi- cation, and in it he expresses a very significant truth about giving.

"My people and I cannot really give you anything, because everything is a gift from you; and we have only given back what is yours already." (verse 14) In verse 11 he had already expressed this principle: *"Everything in heaven and earth is yours, and you are King, supreme ruler over all. All riches and wealth come from you."*

This changes my ideas of giving. When I realize that I really own nothing, but God owns it all, and lets me manage it – then my "giving" takes on a different perspective. What matters now is how responsibly I use all that God has given me – not just what portion of it that I give back.

I CANNOT REALLY GIVE TO GOD

Lord, everything that is, You own,
In heaven and on earth,
All wealth and riches come from You,
And everything of worth.

I really cannot give to You
A thing I do not own,
For everything I may possess
Has come from You alone.

So, when I give, I just return
What is already Yours;
The way You amply meet my need
My meager gift, obscures.

Prayer: *Lord, this has been a hard lesson for me to learn. It has been so easy to think that what I own is mine. Let me never forget that all I have is Yours, and I am responsible for the way I manage it all.*

PRAISE, PROCLAIM, AND MEDITATE

Psalm 145 is a mixture of three things: What "they" will do, what the Lord will do, and what I will do. This is very true-to-life. All of life is made up of what others do, what God does, and what I do.

Since I have little power over what the Lord and others do, I need to concentrate on what I should do. The psalmist, struggling with this, listed seven things he would do:

"I will proclaim your greatness, my God and King." (verse 1)
"I will thank you for ever and ever." (verse 1)
"Every day I will thank you." (verse 2)
"I will praise you for ever and ever." (verse 2)
"I will meditate on your wonderful deeds." (verse 5)
"I will proclaim your greatness." (verse 6)
"I will always praise the Lord." (verse 21)

These seven statements are all summed up in these three areas:

* Praise the Lord
* Proclaim His greatness
* Meditate on His wonderful deeds

PRAISE, PROCLAIM, AND MEDITATE

The psalmist shows me how it's done,
That I should fill my life with praise,
And realize that there is none
But God to whom my praise I raise.

God's greatness also I proclaim
To all on earth who'll pause to hear,
God calls me to exalt His name,
That none on earth may sneer or jeer.

And on God's deeds I meditate,
Aware of all the Lord has done,
From God I will not deviate,
And will not ever shun His Son.

Prayer: *Lord, let me never forget Your greatness and wonderful deeds. Give me the boldness today to proclaim Your greatness, and the readiness to thank You for all that You send my way today – as well as the opportunity to meditate on Your wonderful deeds.*

HOW CAN I GIVE TO THE LORD?

How can I give God anything? Can I give a ten dollar bill, or write a check? Who would the check be payable to? Where would God cash it? We talk about giving to the Lord – giving our tithe and the "first-fruits of our increase." But how do we do it?

Paul gives us an insight into this dilemma in Philippians 4:18. Here he thanks the church for their generosity in sending him so many things by way of Epaphroditus – things he needed so he could survive in a Roman jail. Then he adds that their gifts were like a sweet-smelling offering to God, a sacrifice acceptable to the Lord.

Whether they thought of those gifts to Paul as gifts to God, we do not know. But Paul let them know that such giving was indeed a gift to the Lord.

So – how do we give to God? By giving to meet the needs of people. By giving to enable the Lord's servants to carry on their ministry.

Jesus also gives us this concept in His comment to the effect that whatever we do to and for His people, even the least of them, we are doing it to and for Him.

HOW CAN I GIVE TO THE LORD?

How can I give to God today?

Can I place money in God's hand?

Or write a check and thus convey

Concern for all the Lord has planned?

I give to God as I give to you,

Aware of your every need,

All such giving is in plain view,

And is pleasing to God indeed.

Prayer: *Lord, help me to be alert today for opportunities to give to meet the needs of Your people, whether they be your prominent servants such as Paul, or the least of Jesus' brethren. And Lord, help me to remember always that such giving is giving to You.*

AMAZED!!

When Jesus calmed the storm on Galilee, only a very few people knew about it. The only persons present were the disciples, and they were an interesting contradiction. On the one hand they woke Jesus up, calling on Him to save them. It is as though they expected Him to do something, but they had no idea what it would be.

On the other hand, when He calmed the storm they were all amazed, and declared to each other: *"What kind of man is this? Even the winds and waves obey him!"* (Matthew 8:27)

How much we are like those disciples! So often our praying is like theirs. We ask God for help and when it comes we are amazed. Maybe an important factor is that the disciples prayed in generalities. All they asked for was, "Lord, save us," and prayed for nothing more specific than that.

What do you suppose they expected? Jesus used the most logical and effective way to do it, and they were all amazed.

AMAZED!!

Have you ever prayed and were amazed
At how the Lord had answered you?
Jesus' disciples in fear were dazed,
With only the storm's waves in view.

They turned to Jesus and called for aid,
Not knowing then what He would do;
He spoke the word and the storm was stayed,
While amazing them through and through.

How often also I do as they!
I ask the Lord to intervene;
I bring my need to God as I pray,
Amazed when the answer is seen.

Prayer: *Lord, give me the faith to expect You to do something when I pray. Let me never be amazed that You answer in a particular way.*

SUCCESS

Our world today is filled with people striving to succeed. How interesting that the "secret of success" is plainly stated in Psalm 1. Verse 3 speaks of people who *"succeed in everything they do."* The preceding statements give the ingredients that make up such success - - - -

Reject the advice of evil men.   (verse 1)

Do not follow the example of sinners.   (verse 1)

Don't join those who have no use for God. (verse 1)

Obey the laws of God.   (verse 2)

Study the Law of the Lord day and night. (verse 2)

All this actually distills down to two things: (1) Have nothing to do with God's enemies, and (2) study and obey God's word. When they both are true in me I will succeed in everything I do.

Although this may not be a part of the formula for success in business, it is the formula for success with the Lord.

SUCCESS

The psalmist writes of people who
Succeed in everything they do;
They're strong like trees right by the stream,
To get ahead, they do not scheme.
Two reasons why they prosper so,
Are principles I need to know;
The first is - - stay away from folk
Who think that God is just a joke.

Mark those who have no use for God,
And do not, in their pathway trod;
Reject advice from evil men,
What e'er they speak, or what they pen.
The second one concerns God's word,
That in their lives it is preferred;
They study it both day and night,
It's truth and power bring delight.

God's word is more than just a text
To read to find what happened next;
It's God's own word to us each day,
It's something that we must obey
I want to be as folks like that,
Successful in all that they're at;
Lord, help me so that, day by day,
What's in Your word, I will obey.

Prayer: *Lord, help me seek the success that really counts, success in Your sight.*

HE DIDN'T EVEN ASK

Did you ever read or hear a story inattentively, and make some unfounded assumptions? I did that with the story in John 5, of Jesus' healing a man who had been ill for 38 years. I had assumed that he was lame or paralyzed, and could not walk. And I had assumed that he wanted to get well.

John simply says that he had been sick for thirty-eight years. When Jesus asked him if he wanted to get well, he did not answer. Instead, he simply gave an excuse to the effect that he had no one to help him. Maybe he was a hypochondriac and enjoyed poor health. Maybe he depended on his illness for support, and was fearful of trying to make it on his own.

Here is an example of Jesus' being unwilling to let a person wallow in his own self-pity. He broke up the man's pity party, and told him to get up and do something.

And when he obeyed, it made all the difference in the world. He became well!

HE DIDN'T EVEN ASK

That sick man by Bethesda's pool
Did not ask to be healed
When Jesus saw him there that day,
And by his side had kneeled.

Instead, he gave a lame excuse
For being sick so long,
As though he liked it there amid
That lame and sickly throng.

But Jesus changed his life that day,
And said to him: "Arise
Get up and take your mat along.
Get up and exercise."

So he got up and walked away,
First time in many years;
He went right to the Temple and
Praised God 'mid joyful tears.

But still he did not even ask
The Lord to heal that day,
How fortunate it was for him,
That Jesus passed his way!

Prayer: *Lord, deliver me from self pity. Let that same power that brought healing to that man so long ago, bring power in my life today.*

THE SECRET

A major emphasis of Ephesians is that the wall between Jew and Gentile has been removed, and that God accepts both on an equal basis. In Ephesians 3 Paul gives two paragraphs to the subject, with his main point being that God had this secret plan all the time, but it was just then revealed. Verse 6 identifies that secret - - -

"The secret is that by means of the gospel the Gentiles have a part with the Jews in God's blessings; they are members of the same body and share in the promise that God made through Jesus Christ."

What a long time to keep a secret – from the time of Abraham to Paul! Yet, scattered through the Old Testament are hints of it as though God hoped Israel would figure it out – hints such as:

> The law provided for benefits to strangers who lived within Israel's gates.

> Israel was to be a kingdom of priests to all the nations.

> The earth is the Lord's – *and all they who dwell therein.*

No one saw it until it was revealed to Paul. It was God's eternal purpose, and it seems that He wanted us to figure it out all by ourselves. It is the basis of world wide missions.

THE SECRET

I wonder why God kept it
A secret year by year,
So that the Jewish nation
Just could not see it clear.

God's purpose from the very start
Included more than Jew;
Not only seed of Abraham,
But Gentiles such as you.

The Lord gave them some brains, you know,
To figure all this out;
But their unfounded prejudice
Just kept the Jews in doubt.

So finally after Jesus came,
It was revealed to Paul;
This secret of the ages,
That God accepts us all.

That's the gospel's heart, my friend,
And it's GOOD NEWS indeed,
That both the Jews and Gentiles too
From sin now can be freed.

Prayer: *Lord, thank You for revealing this secret, and making it clear that the gospel of Jesus is for everyone in the world. Thank You that it has meant me too.*

FAITH IN THE FUTURE

All those who have read much in the Bible recognize Hebrews 11 as the chapter of faith. One of the characteristics of these people of faith is that they looked ahead to see the future with confidence in their Lord, rather than look back and dwell on the past.

Noah, Abraham, Isaac, Joseph, and Moses are all described as men whose faith led them to face the future confidently, even though that future was so uncertain

"It was faith that made Noah hear God's warning **about things in the future** *he could not see. ... Abraham was* **waiting for the city** *which God has designed and built , the city with permanent foundations. ... It was faith that made Isaac promise* **blessings for the future** *of Jacob and Esau. ... It was faith that made Joseph, when he was about to die,* **speak of the departure** *of the Israelites from Egypt. ... Moses reckoned that to suffer for the Messiah was worth far more than all the treasures of Egypt, for* **he kept his eyes on the future reward.**

Faith pointed them to the future. It does the same for us today.

FAITH IN THE FUTURE

Faith keeps on looking far ahead,
And not at things gone by;
The unknown turf, it does not dread
But views with wistful eye.

It seeks the new, adventurous life,
Anticipates the new,
Cuts off the past, as with a knife,
And looks to future's view.

Faith is not bound by what's been done,
Unfettered by the past;
It looks to battles not yet won,
The future is a BLAST!

Sometimes I've thought that faith looks back
To a previous, glorious day,
But faith like that is way off track,
It's looking the wrong way.

Prayer: *Lord, as great as the past has been with You, and as great as this present time is now, help me to look ahead to the future with You. Let my faith give me optimism.*

A LOSER'S FAITH

Whenever we hear a sermon or a lesson on Hebrews 11, it almost always lifts up the virtues of such men of great faith as Abel, Enoch, Noah, Abraham, Isaac, Jacob, Joseph, and Moses. All of these were great heroes – great winners. We are admonished that it was their faith that made them great, and faith can do the same for us.

But if that's all we get from Hebrews 11, we miss a great lesson. This chapter also lists a number of losers who had faith too. In verses 35-37 we read of those who died under torture, were mocked and whipped, put in chains and taken off to prison, were stoned, sawed in two, or killed by the sword.

Maybe the point here is that faith is for winners and losers alike. Whether we are on the top or on the bottom, faith is an important ingredient in life. It won't guarantee success, nor will it bring defeat. But in either case it gives us direction in life and hope that keeps on going.

After listing the great heroes and the many "losers," the writer to the Hebrews says, in 11:39: *"What a record all of these have won by their faith!"*

A LOSER'S FAITH

Losers live by their faith as well,
Not only those on top;
Those whose life just seems to be hell,
Are not a great big flop

Faith is not a guarantee
That everything goes well,
That only good will come to me,
And that I will excel.

I show my faith when I am down,
While even in despair;
Though on my face I wear a frown,
And burdened down with care.

Faith gives to me a longer view,
Amid such daily woe;
It helps me push my way on through,
And in defeat – to grow.

Prayer: *Lord, I sometimes have felt that faith is a gimmick to guarantee me the success in life that I seek. Now I see that faith is a stabilizing power no matter if I succeed or not. Whether I am a winner or a loser, help me to have a strong faith in You.*

WHAT GOD DOES NOT DO

We learn to praise by reading and living the Psalms. Psalm 103 is one of those PRAISE psalms, calling the angels and all people to join in praising the Lord. Verses 3-13 give four reasons for such praise:

   a) – We praise for what God is now doing (verses 3-4)

   b) – We praise for what God has already done (vs.6-8)

   c) – We praise for what God does not do (verses 9-10)

   d) – We praise for who God is   (verses 11-13)

WE often praise for what God does, has already done, and for who God is. God forgives – heals –sustains life – shows mercy and love. God fills our lives with good things – judges in favor of the oppressed – and has always been slow to anger and full of mercy.

But what about praising for what the Lord does not do? God does not keep on rebuking. We all know how annoying that kind of nagging can be. God does not hold anger forever. In fact, the Lord forgets our sin once it is forgiven, and does not punish us as we deserve.

Give praise for what God *does not* do!

WHAT GOD DOES NOT DO

We praise the Lord for what He does,
We praise for who He is;
We praise him for his patience too,
And for that love of His.

How often have we thought to praise
For what God does not do?
We've often only thought of that
Which comes within our view.

God does not hold His anger long,
Rebuking o'er and o'er;
Nor punish us as we deserve,
Until we're beat and sore.

Praise God for all He does each day,
For blessings that accrue;
But now I also praise Him for
The things He does not do!

Prayer: *Lord, I praise You for who You are, for what You have done in the past, and for what You are doing now. But today I especially praise You for what You do not do – that You don't nag me, and that You hold Your anger forever. Most of all I praise You for the fact that You do not give me the punishment that I deserve.*

FILLING MY EVERY NEED

Have you ever been bothered by the fact that so much of our praying is self-centered, greedy, and selfish? We pick the statements of scripture (often out of context) that assure us of God's eagerness to fill our every want. We love statements such as *"My God will supply your every need,"* and *"Ask what you will and it will be done."* It is a short step from that, to feeling that God owes it to me, to do what I want Him to.

The writer to the Hebrews gives us a closing prayer and benediction in 13:20-21. As a part of that prayer is this petition: *"May the God of peace provide you with every good thing you need in order to do his will."*

Here is a great insight into the reason to pray such a prayer, and why the Lord might be interested in providing us with every good thing. **It is to enable us to do God's will !**

Maybe the reason why so many prayers go unanswered is that we are not willing to use the answer to help us do the Lord's will. Today when we pray that God provide us with everything we need, let's first figure out how we will use it to do His will.

FILLING MY EVERY NEED

I often ask the Lord above
To fill my every need;
But now I wonder why He should
Hear such a prayer of greed.

The Bible tells me why such prayer
Should e'er be prayed at all;
Not just because I have a need
Is why on God I call.

My every need God will provide
So I can do His will;
Not just so I can possess more,
And live in my greed still.

Prayer: *Lord, forgive my selfishness and greed. I realize that so often I have prayed for something just because I wanted it, and not that it was something I needed in doing Your will.*

ABIDING

Jesus had an intimate, caring, significant conversation with His disciples the night before His crucifixion. It is recorded in John 15. He talked to them about abiding in Him. Some translations use the word, remain, but the King James Version calls it abide. Perhaps no single English word can carry all its meaning.

To remain with Christ, or to abide in Him must mean to be at home with Him, to relax in His presence, to depend on Him, to be open and free in relationships with Him, to trust him, to be willing to let Him know all about me, to love Him, and to draw strength from Him.

When such a relationship prevails, there are several results: I will then bear much fruit (verse 5) – and my prayers will be answered (verse 7).

And verse 10 tells me that such abiding with Christ begins as I obey Him – *"If you obey my commands you will remain in my love just as I have obeyed my Father's commands and remain in His love."*

ABIDING

Lord, teach me so that I abide
In Christ, and that He live inside,
That with His will I not collide,
But that my will, He over-ride.

I want, Oh, Lord, to open wide
My life to You – that I not hide
A thing, but in Your grace reside,
And that Your love be multiplied.

May it be true that I have died
To self and all its sinful pride,
That life in You be ratified,
And that Your Spirit be my guide.

This now is something I decide,
With You, I wish to be allied,
Not merely that it be implied,
I wish in You, Lord, to abide.

Prayer: *Lord, I want to abide in Christ; I want to bear fruit for Him. Help me along that pathway today, as I seek to obey His commands.*

GOD'S PRIMARY MISSION

Amos is the Old Testament preacher of civil rights and justice. In that role, he gives insights into the heart of God concerning the responsibilities that we have to the poor.

One of God's major projects in both the Old and New Testaments was to see that the poor are helped, and that their rights are protected. It was a prominent part of Jesus' good news – that help is on the way to the poor.

God very rarely (if ever) intervenes directly, but instead, instructs us to do it for Him. Since we are so full of greed and self interest ourselves, we often compound the problem rather than solve it. Maybe that is why Jesus taught so much about money and our attitude toward it.

After all these years of such a strong emphasis from God, what is the church doing to help the poor, and to secure their rights? Really not very much! Is this pronouncement of judgement spoken by Amos still valid? *"You are doomed, you that twist justice and cheat people out of their rights."* (Amos 5:7)

GOD'S PRIMARY MISSION

Throughout the scriptures – Old and New,
The poor are God's major concern,
This one thing we're told to do:
For justice for the poor to yearn.

To pray for this is not enough,
The Lord expects us to act,
Words so often are so much fluff,
And only thought in abstract.

When our own greed gets in the way,
We cannot see another's need;
The Lord must see us with dismay,
Consumed as we are with our greed.

Is there, Oh Lord, the slightest hope
That today Your mission I'll see?
Those now at the end of their rope
Are looking for help from me.

Prayer: *Lord, let me be alert to ways I can help bring justice to Your people, the poor. Sensitize me to others' needs – and deliver me from the tyranny of greed.*

GOD ADDED DAY BY DAY

The new church in Jerusalem that grew out of the Holy Spirit's coming must have been quite a dynamic fellowship. The final statement of Acts 2 describes a church that people of all ages since, have yearned for. *"And every day the Lord added to their group those who were being saved."*

Could that be true of churches these days? This paragraph (Acts 2:44-47) lists the characteristics of those people and their church. Maybe the Lord still honors such faith:

> *"All the believers continued together in close fellowship."* (2:44)
> *"They shared their belongings with one another."* (2:44)
> They sold their property and would *"distribute the money among all, according to what each one needed."* (2:45)
> *"Day after day they met as a group in the Temple."* (2:46)
> *"They had their meals together in their homes."* (2:46)
> *"They spent their time praising God."* (2:47)

Is this the formula for church growth today too? When those conditions prevailed in Jerusalem, the Lord added daily those who were being saved.

GOD ADDED DAY BY DAY

Every day God added more,
So that the little church then grew;
Why did the Lord, such power pour
Upon that church, so new?

They let God's power do its work
In miracles divine;
Their part in this they did not shirk,
Nor say – "All this is mine."

They opened up the heart and purse,
And gave their funds away,
In praise and fellowship immersed,
They gathered every day.

Such a spirit will attract
New people day by day;
'Tis then that growth will be a fact,
Instead of slow decay.

Prayer: *Lord, help me learn from history, how You blessed Your church in days gone by. Help me see that my present day life-style of selfishness gets in the way of church growth. Give me the spirit of sharing and worship that the Jerusalem church had back then.*

NOT IN CHAINS

Some of Paul's most inspiring writings came from his experience in Roman prisons. In 2 Timothy 2 he advises Timothy about being willing to discipline himself for the sake of the gospel. He refers to the fact that he himself suffered for the gospel's sake, and was in chains like a common criminal.

Then he makes a great, victorious statement in verse 9 – *"But the word of God is not in chains!"* There is no power in the universe that is strong enough to put God's word in bondage.

The word of God is a liberating, freeing power that emancipates people from the bondage of sin, guilt and judgement. It is a power that the devil can neither control nor defeat. In fact, by it we are able to make Satan back down.

The enemy may be able to bind believers, and put the church in chains temporarily, but no one is strong enough to hold back the word of God!

NOT IN CHAINS

There is no power here on earth,
No power in Heaven above
That e'er can chain the word of God,
Or stop my Father's love.

The ones who bring God's word to men
May suffer for His sake,
But nothing in God's universe
Can His word's power break.

The word of God is powerful,
It does what God commands,
And after all assaults have come,
It still endures, and stands.

The word of God is not in chains,
It conquers every foe;
No enemy, however strong,
Can God's word overthrow.

Prayer: *Lord, thank You for Your mighty, powerful word, that no other power is able to chain it. I praise You that through Your word I have come to know You and trust You.*

ABUNDANT GRACE

Most of us don't need anyone to tell us much about sin; we know a lot about it first hand. Even so, we are reminded in Romans 5 that sin is universal, affecting and infecting everyone. It has brought death upon all the human race. It constantly increased and is still on the rise.

But verse 20 gives us great encouragement – *"Where sin increased, God's grace increased much more."* The grace of God (His undeserved favor for us) has counteracted sin, and has brought to us the solution to our sin problem.

By God's grace our sin can be forgiven. By grace, forgiven sin is forgotten too. By grace we can become new creatures in Christ. By grace we can become part of God's family.

The good news is that even though sin increases and abounds, Gods grace increases and abounds even more. The destructive power of sin as introduced to humanity through Adam, is counteracted by the redemptive power of God's grace, brought to us by Jesus.

ABUNDANT GRACE

Look around us – we can see
That sin is on the rise;
Just stop to think and you'll agree,
Mankind is not so wise.

We've followed just what Adam did,
We've disobeyed our Lord;
And from God's presence we have hid,
Our lives are in discord.

But then – good news has come our way,
Though we are all in sin,
Though from the Lord we all did stray,
God's grace now takes us in.

Our sin has increased, this is true,
And sin, God does deplore;
But here's good news for us to view:
God's grace has increased more!

Prayer: *Lord, I praise You for Your grace – that where I deserve only condemnation, You have extended forgiveness. Thank You!*

RELATED BY OBEDIENCE

Matthew and Mark each record the episode of Jesus' mother and brothers coming to take Him home as He was speaking to a crowd. They send in word that they wanted to see Him, and His response in each account was: *"Who is my mother, and who are my brothers? Whoever does what my Father in heaven wants him to do is my brother, sister, and mother."* (Matthew 12:49-50, and Mark 3:33-35)

This raises an interesting and challenging question for each of us: Does the way I live show that I am related to Jesus? That seems to be the bottom line on this issue. Is one of the major characteristics of my life the fact that I obey what my Father in heaven wants me to do? A part of Jesus' mission on earth was to get people to obey His Father.

I guess we have lost the concept that true spirituality is best seen in obedience to the Lord's commands – not merely in an orthodox belief.

RELATED BY OBEDIENCE

Can we be related to Christ
As brother, sister, mother too?
Can anyone be close to Him,
And such a relationship review?

The person who obeys his God
And follows what from God he's heard,
Is one related to our Christ,
For he obeys God's holy word.

Relationships that really count
Are based on more than merely blood;
What matters is the faith and trust
That covers o'er us as a flood.

I'm Jesus' brother as I trust
His Father – and as I obey;
To demonstrate that we're related,
There is no other better way.

Prayer: *Jesus, deliver me from dry and dead orthodoxy, and lead me into a life style of obedience – obedience to all that Your Father tells me to do.*

FILL ME WITH YOUR WILL

A great insight in prayer is found in Colossians 1:9, as Paul prays for that church: *"We ask God to fill you with the knowledge of his will, with all the wisdom and understanding that His Spirit gives."*

This is the foundation for a number of other accomplishments. When such a prayer as this is answered in my life, then verse 10 indicates that - - - -

--- I can live as the Lord wants me to,

--- I will always do what pleases the Lord,

--- My life will produce all kinds of good deeds,

--- I will grow in my knowledge of God.

So often we go about this backwards. We try to live as God wants us to without fully knowing what He wants. Paul's prayer tells us how all this can be achieved. When God fills us with the knowledge of His will, these four conditions described in verse 10 will follow.

FILL ME WITH YOUR WILL

My basic prayer is this, O Lord:
That I might know Your will,
That knowledge of just what You want,
My mind and soul will fill.

'Tis then that I could live, O Lord,
Just as You want me to;
And only that which pleases You
Is what I'll always do.

To know Your will, will bring to me
All kinds of good deeds done;
And I will grow in knowing You,
In living for Your Son.

So – show to me Your will, O Lord,
Is what I pray today;
Lord, fill my mind with what You want,
And lead me in Your way.

Prayer: *Lord, I really want to do Your will, but don't always recognize what it is. Fill me with an understanding of your will today.*

THAT THEY MAY BE ONE

Jesus prayed fervently for the disciples whom He had chosen and trained. John 17 records His earnest prayer for their safety and perseverance, pleading that the enemy would not get control of them.

But He also prayed for us that night. In verse 29 He said: *"I pray not only for them but also for those who believe in me because of their message."* We who believe today are in that prayer, for we have believed because of the message of the disciples.

For us, He prayed one thing: that we may all be one, completely one (verses 21, 23). He also gave a specific reason for such a prayer – *"So that the world will believe that you sent me ... in order that the world may know that you sent me, and that you love them as you love me."*

It has been said that the greatest scandal in the church of today is the way we have divided into little factions, and refuse to work or fellowship together. Jesus prayed that such division would not come to pass.

THAT THEY MAY BE ONE

The way we often fret and fuss,
And fight within the church,
Will show the world those sins in us,
That Jesus' name besmirch.

He prayed that all of us be one,
That all divisions go;
That all who follow God's own Son,
Such unity will show.

But what have we done through the years?
We squabble and we fight;
We've caused our Lord so many tears,
To Him, we're no delight.

Our lack of unity, you see,
Will keep non-Christians out;
With God, they never will agree,
If this great prayer, we doubt.

Prayer: *Lord, forgive me for my part in the scandalous divisions in today's church. I know You grieve when Your body is fractured like that. Help me to be a part of a unifying power in Your church.*

MY FATHER SEES

Jesus emphasized a difference in piety from that which was practiced by the Pharisees. In Matthew 6:4, 6, 18. He speaks of that difference in alms-giving, prayer, and fasting. Regarding each of these three disciplines, He states a principle:

"And your Father, who sees what you do in private will reward you."

This must be an important truth or He would not have said it three times. It is, of course, a contrast to the Pharisees, who were so public with all their religious practices.

It has been so easy to miss the point here. We have often been taught that this is merely a tirade against Pharisees. But Jesus' bottom line in it all was the positive statement that the God who sees what we do in private will reward us.

The main concern then, is what we do in private. Do we give, pray, and fast? And do we do these because it is right to do so, or so that others will think better of us?

After all – it is really what God sees that counts.

MY FATHER SEES

My Lord can see all that I do,
He knows all that I am;
He understands me through and through,
He knows when I'm a sham.

He sees my fasting, alms, and prayer,
He sees all that I do;
No need to openly declare
These things to others' view.

He sees what I do, wrong or right,
Standing, or if I fall;
He knows me – I am in His sight,
To Him, I trust it all.

Prayer: *Lord, I know You see everything I do – but at times I so easily forget it. Remind me throughout this day that You see all I do in private. Even though others do not see, and do not know, I thank You that You do.*

ANANIAS AND SAPPHIRA TODAY

The Jerusalem church embarked on quite an experiment in communal living, as described in Acts 4 and 5. Each person sold possessions and brought the money to be a part of a common treasury which was then used to meet the needs of each family.

We don't know if this was in obedience to God's leading – or if it was strictly a human experiment, but they certainly must have thought it was the proper thing to do.

How interesting that this brought about the first controversy and tension in this new church! It came in the form of greed and pretense. When Ananias and Sapphira saw how the church praised the generosity of Barnabas and others, they decided that they wanted to be the center of such attention too. But their greed soon got the upper hand. They pretended that they were giving all their assets, while holding back some of it for their own use.

Judgment on such deception was harsh and swift, as both of them were struck dead. How fortunate that the Lord no longer delivers such prompt punishment! Who of us would survive to tell the story?

ANANIAS AND SAPHIRA TODAY

We meet them in the church today,
They seem to have a lot to say;
They now go by a different name,
But attitudes are still the same.

They boast of all the cash they give
And of the pious lives they live;
Their faith in God is mostly talk,
Not much commitment in their walk.

When first they came upon the scene,
The Lord stepped in to intervene,
So that Sapphira fell down dead
As Ananias went on ahead.

What if the Lord did this today,
And punished sin without delay?
Who of us would then be spared,
If war on sin were thus declared?

Prayer: *Lord, so often I have acted just as Ananias and Sapphira did. As with them, my greed too, gets in the way of my giving. Deliver me from this sin, I pray.*

BARNABAS

After Saul of Tarsus was converted he experienced quite a bit of frustration at being rejected by the Jerusalem Christians. Acts 9:26 tells what happened when he reported to them. *"Saul went to Jerusalem and tried to join the disciples. But they would not believe that he was a disciple, and they were all afraid of him."* Of course they were afraid – he had tried to stamp out their faith.

He learned early in his new life as a believer, that he reaped just what he had planted. He had sown violence, threats, persecution and death, and now found that he was reaping opposition.

But then someone came into his life to change all that. He met Barnabas, who came to his rescue and took him to the disciples, explaining how he had been dramatically converted, and that now he was an eloquent preacher of the gospel.

What a difference one person makes! What an encouragement Barnabas was! That's what his name means – **son of encouragement.** We certainly need more like Barnabas today, those who will believe the best in people, and be an encouragement.

BARNABAS

Is Barnabas now still around,
Whose presence is to cheer?
Can any like him still be found,
Encouragingly near?

When I'm thrown out – not understood,
It's Barnabas I need;
An intercessor, one who could
My case to others plead.

Am I a Barnabas as well?
Do I stand by a friend,
So doubts about him I dispel,
As my support I lend?

Prayer: *Lord, thank You for all the Barnabas-type people who have encouraged me along life's way. Help me today to be a Barnabas to someone who needs encouragement.*

TWO – WAY FAITH

The account of Peter and Cornelius in Acts 10 is a story of close timing and two-way faith. When God appeared to Cornelius and told him to contact Peter, Peter was still all bound up in his Jewish prejudices against Gentiles.

The Lord was counting on Peter to have changed by the time Corneluis could contact him. God had faith in Peter, and depended on him to have changed his attitude by the time the messengers reached him.

In the meantime, while those messengers were on their way, God worked on Peter. It all depended on Peter's ability to change, and the Lord had the faith that he would. It was close timing, since Peter was at the point of change just as the messengers arrived.

Does the Lord still work this way, and get in touch with us to open our minds to new opportunities of obedience, just as those opportunities are developing? This probably happens more often that we imagine, and if we fail – God's work in other people's lives is frustrated.

TWO - WAY FAITH

Faith seems like a two-way street,
Where those who trust each other meet;
Just as we may trust the Lord,
And have obedience explored,
So the Lord depends on us
To follow Him without a fuss.

Here's a truth I've come to see:
Sometimes the Lord shows faith in me,
If I'm open to His will,
His purpose then I can fulfil;
If to Him I close my mind,
Some other channel He must find.

Prayer: Lord, help me respond promptly to Your leading today. You may be depending on me today to bring Your message of good news and cheer to someone; and if I fail You, it just may not get done.

OPEN TO THE NEW

The new church in Jerusalem, as described in the early chapters of Acts, was a refreshing thing to behold. They were wide open to new ideas, new challenges, new concepts, and new ways of doing things.

When Peter came back from meeting with the Roman Centurion, Cornelius, the church leaders said: *"You were a guest in the house of uncircumcised Gentiles, and you even ate with them!"* What a damaging accusation! It was enough to throw Peter out of the fellowship.

But when he explained, they listened; as Acts 11, verse 18 says: *"they stopped their criticism, and praised God."*

Think what could happen in churches today if we had similar openness to new possibilities. So often our standard position is: "We've never done it that way before."

OPEN TO THE NEW

"We've never done like that before!"
We hear so often o'er and o'er;
Thank God that early church did not
Upon that worn-out saying, squat.

Their minds were open to the new,
To see all that the Lord could do;
If their traditions did not fit,
Then to the new ways they'd submit.

Refreshing was that church back then,
To brand-new ways they said, "Amen!"
How sad that churches of today
Are set in ways like fired clay.

Prayer: *Lord, deliver me from such traditionalism that makes me deaf to Your leading. Let me see the new things that You want to do today through Your church.*

THE LORD'S ENDURANCE

Most of Acts 13 is Paul's sermon, delivered at one of his stops on the first missionary journey. To illustrate his point, he re-caps some of Israel's history with the Lord. Verse 18 (in the Today's English Version) records him saying: *"And for forty years He endured them in the desert."* Even though a footnote gives an alternative reading, *"He took care of them," this is an intriguing thought.*

The Lord did indeed endure a lot from Israel in the desert:

> He endured their disobedience,
> He endured their idolatry,
> He endured their rebellion,
> He endured their complaining,
> He endured their ingratitude.

How is it with the church today? Does the Lord still endure his saints? Not much has changed since then, for we today grieve the Lord in much the same ways.

What must the Lord endure in me these days?

THE LORD'S ENDURANCE

The Lord endures a lot, my friend,
As in the desert, long ago
His patience seems to have no end,
How far will his endurance go?

They turned to idols, disobeyed,
And showed no gratitude at all;
I marvel how God's wrath was stayed,
For on them, judgement did not fall.

Since then it has not changed a lot
For we today are much the same;
Rebellion still is quite a blot
On us who claim to take God's name.

I wonder how long He'll endure
The sin in which today we live;
How long can we feel so secure,
When Israel's sin we still re-live?

Prayer: *Lord, I know that in many ways I have grieved You, and that You endure me and my sins just as You endured Israel. Help me to adopt a life-style that You will approve, not just endure.*

GOD'S CHOSEN PEOPLE TODAY

It was not easy for the young Christian church in Jerusalem to be Christian, instead of an extension of Judaism. To settle this issue, they called a church council. Acts 15 reports it. The main issue was: must Gentile believers submit to all the Jewish rituals and laws to be Christian?

This was hotly debated, and James makes an interesting observation in verse 14: *"God first showed His care for the Gentiles by taking from them a people to belong to Him."* What an interesting twist! The selection of the Jews was God's expression of care for all the other nations of the world.

Does this mean also that today when God selects a person to be saved, that it is an expression of divine care for all people not yet committed to Him? Just as the whole world, so we are chosen to be redeemed so we can be a "kingdom of priests" to the rest of the world.

We are the chosen people of God for this generation!

GOD'S CHOSEN PEOPLE TODAY

Israel missed the point back then,
When chosen by the Lord;
They thought that since they were so good,
This then was God's reward.

But God had called them for His use,
As tools in His hand,
To spread the news of His great love
To folks in every land.

Instead, they turned their faith within,
Neglecting God's own call;
They thought that they were better than
The Gentiles, one and all.

How odd that that same feeling now
Exists in God's own church!
We often go our merry way
And leave God in the lurch.

Prayer: *Lord, forgive me for the times I have neglected this truth, and for the times I have failed to be Your link with others. Lead me to the people today for whom I am to be Your priest.*

IN THAT PHILIPPIAN JAIL

The episode of Paul and Silas being arrested, whipped, jailed and then released, in Acts 16, raises a long list of questions.

What did they pray for in the prison that night? Did they plead for release and justice, or was it praise only? How could they sing under such painful circumstances? How did the other prisoners feel about their unusual and odd behavior? Were other prisoners saved too, as a result of their singing and praying?

It would have been so natural for Paul and Silas to complain, to demand their rights, or even to plot revenge. Why do we find it so difficult to learn from such events as this? Why do we still respond with violence, threats, or revenge?

Why do we find it so hard to pray and praise in unfair and difficult situations?

IN THAT PHILIPPIAN JAIL

Their feet in stocks, with beaten backs,
As though oppressed by maniacs,
Confined in prison, late that night,
They found themselves in awful plight.

Paul and Silas in that jail,
Decided not to rant and rail;
Nor did they give up in despair,
Instead, they looked to God in prayer.

We know not that for which they prayed,
As there confined in that stockade;
No doubt for self they did not pray,
Or that their troubles go away.

For answers in advance they praised,
In gratitude, their voices raised;
God heard their praise, and answered prayer,
God showed them power then and there.

I wonder – will I learn from this,
Or will it's lesson I dismiss?
When everything in life goes wrong,
Will I respond with prayer and song?

Prayer: *Lord, I want to be like Paul and Silas, but I don't have the strength. I pray today for the ability to sing and praise when life gets tough.*

TO BE GREAT

The mother of James and John was such a typical mom! In her strong desire for the best for her sons, she asked Jesus to give them special places of honor in His Kingdom. But her meddling caused more problems than it solved. The other disciples became angry, and the group was divided. That scenario sounds familiar, doesn't it?

Their anger is not so surprising; they probably did not want James and John to get the jump on them, and thus have an advantage over the rest. Maybe they were angry because none of them had thought of doing something like that. Maybe they resented the fact that a mother had made such a request for her sons.

However it developed, Jesus defused the tension by talking to them about how a person becomes great in His kingdom – namely by serving. He said: *"If one of you wants to be great, he must be the servant of the rest."* (Matthew 20:27)

Now there's a lesson that we still struggle with, and struggle against. Who wants to be great that way?

TO BE GREAT

If someone wishes to be great,
And at the top would relocate –

If over others he would rate,
If his desire is to dictate –

There's just one way he'd elevate
To that place where he'd dominate –

And that is if he'd abdicate
All his ambition to be great.

Prayer: *Lord, teach me this lesson. Take away any desire that I have to dominate others. Let me learn how to serve, O Lord – and whether or not I ever become great is then beside the point.*

THAT MACEDONIAN CALL

Paul's decision to enter Europe by way of Macedonia in Greece gives us an interesting insight into the way God calls His servants to new fields. Acts 16:10 tells it: *"We decided that God had called us to preach the good news to people there."*

But there is no evidence or record that God had spoken to them, or that the Spirit was pushing them to go into Macedonia. No opening or closing of doors, as was the case when the Spirit prevented them from going into Asia minor or Bithynia earlier.

How had God called them to Macedonia? All there was, was a vision of a man saying, *"Come over to Macedonia and help us."* (Acts 16:9) Is that all that is needed to constitute a call from God? Are all pleas from people in need, actually the call of the Lord?

Does God still extend calls like that today? The majority of such calls are not even heard, because we so easily turn a deaf ear to the needs of others.

THE MACEDONIAN CALL

'Twas just a Macedonian man
In vision of the night;
But in the mind of Paul, 'twas more,
It was the Lord's invite.

Whenever there is human need,
The Lord Himself dwells there;
Such need becomes a call to us:
"Come over here, and share."

We need no further call from God
To carry out His will;
Whenever we see human need,
That need we're called to fill.

The Lord is present in each one
Who suffers anywhere;
This might be all the call God gives,
Just meet the Lord in prayer.

Prayer: *Lord, have You been calling me all this time, and I have not heard? Help me to be sensitive to the needs of people all around, and let me hear Your voice in theirs.*

THAT YOUR LOVE WILL KEEP ON GROWING

As Paul began his letter to the Philippians, he expresses his basic prayer for that church. After sharing the prayer in verse 9, he describes the lifestyle that would result when the prayer becomes a reality.

The prayer is that their love will keep on growing more and more, and that it be mingled with true knowledge and perfect judgment. Then in 1:10-11 he describes the life style that would develop - - - -

"You will be able to choose what is best." (verse 10)

"You will be free from all impurity." (verse 10)

"You will be free from all blame." (verse 10)

"Your lives will be filled with the truly good qualities which only Jesus can produce." (verse 11)

That is quite an impressive four point goal statement for Christian living! The strategy to reach this goal is being filled with a love that keeps on growing more and more.

THAT YOUR LOVE WILL KEEP ON GROWING

Paul prayed that my love grow and grow,
And with it, that much more I know,
That perfect judgment will be mine;
Those three requests he did combine.

If these be true in how I live,
Then this additional additive
Will be a part of my life style;
And on my conduct, God will smile.

I'll be empowered to choose the best,
And be able too – to pass God's test;
I'll from impurities be free,
And God will place no blame on me.

My life will be all filled with good,
I'll be in Christ just what I should;
All this results as my love grows,
For a love like that really shows.

Prayer: *Lord, I want that kind of love in my life. I pray that such a love for You and for people will keep on growing more and more.*

A GREAT AMERICAN HERESY

In Philippians 1:27, Paul writes of the Christian life style: *"Now the important thing is that your way of life should be as the Gospel of Christ requires."*

The "in thing" in Christian life style in America is an emphasis on the gospel of health and wealth – that God really desires to give us all a life of ease, prosperity, and success. This is a primary message of many radio and TV evangelists these days.

Maybe we are in the midst of a great American heresy. We've turned the gospel inside out, so that the focus is on our wants, not on what our Lord wants. Paul expressed it in a very un-American way in verse 29: *"For you have been given the privilege of serving Christ, not only by believing in him, but also by suffering for him."*

Instead of that, we are told that if we have seed faith, God will prosper us beyond belief; and with possibility thinking, God will hand deliver to us everything that we ask for. We are told that His main business is giving us prosperity and health.

But Paul wrote of suffering for Christ!

A GREAT AMERICAN HERESY

The gospel that was preached by Paul
Was different from today's;
He preached that Christ was all-in-all,
And He deserves our praise.

A different gospel now I hear,
With focus on my need;
They tell me just be of good cheer,
And give to God a seed.

Then God will cause that seed to grow,
So I'll have all I seek;
I never will run short of dough,
Life never will be bleak.

The gospel now preached in our land,
Puts man upon the throne;
It says, "God's here to lend a hand,
Whenever we might groan."

Prayer: *Lord, I'm confused by what I hear preached these days. I do want to see Your power in my life, but if that must be through suffering, then let Your power and presence be very obvious.*

KEEP ON IMITATING ME

Paul expressed his philosophy of life in Philippians 3:12-14. It includes some very significant principles:

> I do not claim that I have already succeeded.
>
> I do not claim that I have already become perfect.
>
> I keep striving to win the prize.
>
> The one thing I do is to forget what is behind me.
>
> I do my best to reach what is ahead.
>
> I run straight toward the goal.

Then, a few sentences later he urges – *"Keep on imitating me."* (verse 17) Such a statement raises a few questions for us today.

> Was it arrogant for Paul to set himself up as an example for others?
> Are we today to live just as Paul did then?
> In what particular aspects should we imitate him?

Instead of arrogance, maybe it was Paul's sincere desire that they (and we) might know Christ as he did.

KEEP ON IMITATING ME

"I am the one to imitate,"
Is just what Paul wrote them;
What traits am I to cultivate,
And what should I condemn?

Should I adopt Paul's trait to boast,
And brag on what I've done?
What should I imitate the most,
And what things should I shun?

There are some traits I see in Paul
I'd like to see in me;
Concern for people, great and small,
That Christ would set them free.

The zeal with which he loved the Lord,
The fearless way he preached,
When even held by Roman sword,
So many folks he reached.

I thank God for a man like Paul,
Who showed us how to live;
In all of time he stands so tall,
And so provocative.

Prayer: *Lord, I thank You for such a role-model as Paul. May the same zeal and excitement for the gospel – and concern for people, be a part of me.*

FAITH, HOPE, AND LOVE

When Paul prayed for the Thessalonian church, he added, *"We remember how you put your <u>faith</u> into practice, how your <u>love</u> made you work so hard, and how your <u>hope</u> in our Lord is firm."* (I Thes. 1:3) When he wrote to Corinth he lifted love above faith and hope, and gave it more importance. But here he makes no comparison. He treats all three equally.

Faith, love and hope are far more inter-related than we have thought. When I put faith into practice it shows in my love and hope. Love is right in the middle of it all. A firm hope is built on active faith and love. Each of these three qualities contributes to the strengthening of the other two

> Faith helps my love and hope to grow,
> Love helps my hope and faith to grow,
> Hope helps my love and faith to grow,
>
> Faith and hope together help my love,
> Love and faith together help my hope,
> Hope and love together help my faith.

No wonder Paul writes in 1 Corinthians 13 — "Meanwhile, these three remain: faith, hope, and love."

FAITH, HOPE, AND LOVE

These three gifts from God above
Have come to fill my life up so,
There's faith and hope, and of course, love,
Each helps the other two to grow.

My faith and love increase my hope,
So that it now is confidence;
No need in hopelessness to mope,
When my God has omnipotence!

My love and hope make my faith grow,
So even mountains can be moved;
When I am in God's power-flow,
I know my faith has been approved.

My hope and faith make my love strong,
And through love, God's a part of me;
He puts within my heart a song,
In gratitude for all these three!

Prayer: *Lord, fill my life, my mind, my soul, and my heart with faith, love, and hope. May they be prominent enough to show.*

SPEAKING AS GOD WANTS ME TO

Shortly after Paul was forced to leave the believers in Thessalonica, he wrote an intimate and personal note to them. One of his statements to them is very appropriate for us today, and gives us a lot to ponder. It is: *"We always speak as God wants us to."* (1 Thes. 2:4) In a few sentences surrounding that state-ment, he expands on it in this way:

"Our appeal to you was not based on error" (2:3)

"Nor was it based on impure motives." (2:3)

"Nor do we try to trick anyone." (2:4)

"We do not try to please men, but God." (2:4)

"We did not come to you with flattering talk." (2:5)

"Nor did we use words to cover up greed." (2:5)

"We did not try to get praise from anyone." (2:6)

What a check list for evaluating our speaking! Am I able to pass all seven of these, and say that they describe the way I speak?

Do I always – or sometimes – or ever, speak as God wants me to?

SPEAKING AS GOD WANTS ME TO

Lord help me watch whate'er I say,
That what I speak throughout this day
Be only that which will convey
That I want You to have Your way.

May what I say be always true,
That no wrong motive misconstrue,
That when I'm speaking, I review,
So all I say is pleasing You.

Don't let my speaking e'er mislead,
So that Your truth it might impede,
Or that it cover up my greed,
Or just ignore some other's need.

Let every word that comes from me
Be that with which You will agree;
Words are important – now I see,
I pray that mine will all please Thee.

Prayer: *Lord, set a guard over my speech, so that I speak only what You would have me say, and in a manner that reflects Your presence in my life.*

JESUS' RETURN

In Paul's writings in the New Testament, we read a lot about Jesus' return to earth – especially in his first letter to the Thessalonians. He draws two basic conclusions from it all, and passes them on as commands. Both are appropriate for us today.

a) This great future event must have an effect on how we live now. We must be sober, awake and alert to God. Our lives must be characterized by faith, love and hope. (1 Thessalonians 5:6-8)

b) We must encourage one another with the assurance of such a great truth as Jesus' return. (1 Thessalonians 4:18 and 5:11)

Much of the preaching on this subject these days is aimed at instilling fear instead of encouragement. Paul does not use this truth as an evangelism weapon, nor does he warn them: "Believe before it is too late." He uses it as an encouragement to believers.

Actually, only believers can appreciate and understand how important and exciting Jesus' return really is.

JESUS' RETURN

Why teach or preach our Lord's return?
Why mention it at all?
Just one reason – so that our faith
And hope and love grow tall.

It's not a truth to frighten us,
That we should live in fear;
But rather to encourage us,
That we, to God, draw near.

Alive or dead when Jesus comes,
What difference does it make?
For everyone who's trusted Him
To Heaven, He will take.

Lord, let this truth encourage me,
And fill my life with hope,
And faith, and love – that each of these
Help me, with life to cope.

Prayer: *Lord, I anticipate Jesus' return with hope and love and faith today. May the expectation of this great event encourage me throughout this day.*

ENCOURAGEMENT!

It was when the Apostle Paul was in Corinth that he was led away from the Jews, and led by God, to go to the Gentiles. At the beginning of his stay there, he received a much-needed encouragement from the Lord in the form of a vision:

"Do not be afraid, but keep on speaking and do not give up, for I am with you. No one will be able to harm you, for many in the city are my people." (Acts 18:9-10)

This is the story of encouragement every minister needs to hear; for it is so easy to become discouraged in ministry these days. The message of that vision strikes at the core of modern-day problems in ministry: FEAR, DISCOURAGEMENT, and INTIMIDATION.

We usually think of a vision as a way for God to convince Paul to move on to some new place. This time the vision was to convince him to stay. Have you prayed lately that your pastor might receive such encouragement from the Lord?

ENCOURAGEMENT!

At just the time I need it most,
When I'm besieged by fear,
'Tis then that God draws near to me,
With what I need to hear.

When I am tempted to give up,
And simply quit it all,
That's when the Lord encourages,
Just as He did with Paul.

When Satan would intimidate,
And threaten me with harm,
That's when the Lord stands by my side,
Removing my alarm.

Prayer: *Lord, I pray for my pastor today. Send a word of encouragement as You did to Paul. If You want to send it through me, help me to be your faithful messenger.*

GIVING AND RECEIVING

Near the end of Paul's third missionary journey, he arranged to meet the elders of the Ephesian church at Miletus, and bid them all farewell. It was a very moving and emotional time for all of them, and a spiritually strengthening experience for the church elders.

Just as he had written to Corinth, so also he reminds these folks – that he had come to them at his own expense, as a preacher who also held a secular job. He explains that his purpose was to demonstrate the principle that by working hard, we will be able to help the weak.

Then, to substantiate that thought, he quotes Jesus as saying: *"There is more happiness in giving than in receiving."* (Acts 20:35)

We do not know where or when Jesus said this, or even how Paul learned of it. But we do know that it certainly is consistent with the total emphasis of Jesus' teaching.

Do you suppose we will ever experience the truth of what Jesus said? Will we ever learn that there is more happiness in giving than in receiving?

GIVING AND RECEIVING

Here's a truth that most of us
Ignore from day to day,
Because the ways in which we live,
Our selfishness betray.

More happiness will come to us
When we learn how to give,
Than ever could accrue to us
When selfishly we live.

"To give is better than to get,"
Is what our Lord had said;
The world tells us the opposite:
"Just live to get instead."

So still we go our merry way,
Just seeking to receive;
We miss the blessings that would come
If this truth we'd believe.

Prayer: *Lord, I confess that it has been difficult for me to grasp the truth of Jesus' saying. I thank You for all You give me; but help me experience the joy and happiness of giving too.*

THE WONDER OF GOD'S GRACE

God's grace (undeserved favor) is something that the human mind cannot fully comprehend. We can almost understand it, but not completely. It is so foreign to our nature that even when we receive it we still don't understand. That's because it is so hard for us to forgive others.

Ephesians 2:1-10 is an exciting section of scripture – describing what God's grace is like, and what it has done for us.

By grace, God gave us life with Christ,

By grace, we have been saved,

By grace, God raised us up with Christ to rule with him in heaven.

By grace, God created us for a life of good deeds.

To extend favor, forgiveness and acceptance when it is not deserved, goes against our nature; but that's exactly what grace is. Verse 7 describes our conversion in terms of God's grace: *"He did this to demonstrate for all time to come the extraordinary greatness of his grace in the love he showed us in Christ Jesus."*

THE WONDER OF GOD'S GRACE

I stood condemned there in my place,
My sin had brought me such disgrace;
Unwilling now my guilt to face,
The word, condemned! had closed my case.

Oh that some power could erase
My sin and guilt – and then replace
Them – leaving not a single trace:
But that would take abundant grace.

As in my mind these yearnings race,
God's love gave me such an embrace;
It filled me so as to displace
My sin, and put God in its place.

Conversion is an "about face,"
So guilt no longer will debase
My soul at such a rapid pace,
Oh – The Wonder of God's Grace!

Prayer: *Lord, I don't understand, but I praise You for Your extraordinary grace. When I least deserve it You extend Your favor, love and forgiveness to me. Thank You!*

PAUL'S PRAYER AND MINE

As Paul wrote to the Ephesian church in 3:16-19, he explains how he had been praying for them:

- ------- that God would give them power (out of the wealth of His glory, and through His Spirit,)

- ------- that Christ would make His home in their hearts,

- ------- that they would have roots and foundations in love,

- ------- that they would understand Christ's love – how broad, long, high, and deep it is, even though it can never be fully known,

- ------- that they be completely filled with God's perfect fullness.

What a prayer this is! Though we may not fully comprehend it, we certainly can identify with it. We can yearn that all of it might be true of us as well. These are really the things we need each day.

What Paul prayed for them, I now pray for myself.

PAUL'S PRAYER AND MINE

All that for which Paul prayed for them,
Are things that I now pray for me;
May this be true within my life
Today, becomes my earnest plea.

That Christ come into me and live,
That He will make my heart His home,
And thus bring power and strength within,
That from His will I shall not roam.

That my whole being shall have roots
In love that really is divine.
And that I comprehend such love,
Until it be completely mine.

Then Lord – if all of this be true,
It means that I'll be filled with Thee;
And that Your perfect fullness dwell
Right here each day inside of me.

Prayer: *Lord, let me experience Your power, Your love, Your fullness. May Christ make His home in my heart*

DO I STILL MEASURE UP?

Paul gives a penetrating challenge to his readers in Ephesians 4:1 – *"I urge you then ... live a life that measures up to the standards God set when he called you."* Then, in the next few statements he gives a series of clues regarding that statement.

"Be always humble, gentle and patient." (4:2)

"Show your love by being tolerant with one another." (4:2)

"Do your best to preserve the unity which the spirit gives by means of the peace that binds you together." (4:3)

In examining myself against such a list as that, I must ask: Am I humble, gentle, patient, helpful, peaceful, and do I preserve unity? Or – could it be true that some of the opposite traits show up? Am I ever arrogant, rough, impatient, demanding, divisive, or belligerent?

What change in my life would take place if I measured up to the standard God set when He called me?

DO I STILL MEASURE UP?

I wonder if I measure up
To standards that God set
When I was first called out of sin,
When first my Lord, I met.

God called me to conform to Christ,
Live out humility;
Be gentle, patient, helpful too,
Preserving unity.

God called me to let love and peace
Pervade my mind and soul —
That all of these great qualities
Show that He's in control.

Is this the measure of my life,
Now that the years have passed?
Does that fresh love still dwell in me?
Have I been that steadfast?

Prayer: *Lord, measure me today by Your measure. I want Your Spirit to do His work in me, to conform me to the standards that You have set.*

FAITH ALONE IS NOT ENOUGH

How much my faith grows, and how I mature as a Christian does not rest on God's ability or willingness to give me strength. Rather, it depends on me. Peter gives us this message in 2 Peter 1, when he urges us to add a few significant qualities to our faith:

It is as though he tells us that faith is not enough. Be sure to add to it. *"... do your best to add goodness to your faith ..."* Then follows a list of proper additives.

Add **knowledge** to your goodness,

Add **self control** to your knowledge,

Add **endurance** to your self control,

Add **godliness** to your endurance,

Add **brotherly** affection to your godliness,

Add **love** to your brotherly affection.

None of this is automatic. It all takes work and a conscious effort; and I am the one who must do the work. When I do this, then verse 10 can be true – that God's call and His choice of me, become a permanent experience.

FAITH ALONE IS NOT ENOUGH

Faith by itself just will not do,
So, other traits I must pursue;
Goodness, knowledge, and self control
Must also overwhelm my soul.

Endurance too, and godliness,
My entire being must express;
Brotherly affection and love
Must also fit me like a glove.

When to my faith I add all these,
'Tis then that I my God can please;
And in my Christian life I'll grow,
While to the world my faith I show.

Prayer: *Lord, I want to add all these qualities to my faith so that Your call to me may become a permanent experience. Help me today to make a conscious effort to do this.*

THE WAR WITHIN ME

That which every Christian knows by experience is described in Romans 7 & 8. There is a war going on within each of us. It is a battle between the Spirit of God and the sinful nature that still lives in us.

Sometimes we ascribe to Paul the status of a "super saint" who has won victory over all such battles. But he describes it well in Romans 7:18-19 - *"I know that good does not live in me – that is, in my human nature. For even though the desire to do good is in me, I am not able to do it. I don't do the good I want to; instead I do the evil that I don't want to."*

This battle is so important that he says in 8:8 – *"Those who obey their human natures cannot please God."*

But he goes on later in chapter 8 to let us know that the solution lies in our conscious effort to let the Spirit of God have control of all that we do.

THE WAR WITHIN ME

There is a war in me today,
Two great powers each wants its way;
My sinful nature wants control,
The Spirit of God seeks my soul.

The battle ground is daily life,
For that is where I sense the strife;
Which of these powers will I obey?
And which will finally fade away?

It's how I live and what I do,
What kind of goals that I pursue;
Do I give in to this world's lust,
And all my human instincts trust?

Or will I let God's Spirit lead?
Will I obey what He's decreed?
The outcome's fully up to me,
For I'm the one in charge, you see.

Prayer: *Lord, I am in the same daily battle that Paul experienced. Help me today to let Your Spirit control my life – my feelings – my emotions – my reactions – my thinking – all my doing.*

TIME

Scattered throughout all scripture are references to eternity, and the fact that God is eternal. Eternity always has been hard for us to comprehend, because we are so bound by time.

Psalm 93 is a brief praise-statement about the Lord. Two sentences (verses 2 & 3) emphasize that He is eternal: *"Your throne, O Lord, has been from the beginning, and you existed before time began. Your laws are eternal, Lord, and your temple is holy indeed for ever and ever."*

We are incapable of thinking of eternity apart from time. We think of it as an endless extension of time, and even sing of that in one of our popular hymns:

When we've been there ten thousand years,
Bright shining as the sun,
We've no less days to sing God's praise
Than when we've first begun.

But there is no such thing as time in eternity, for eternity is the absence of time – an eternal NOW. We even sometimes wonder about people of previous generations who have had to wait so long for the final judgement day. But there can be no waiting either, when there is no time. If we could only comprehend an existence without time, we could understand more about God and eternity.

TIME

Time, to us, is the measure of life,
In minute, hour, and day;
We even try to put God in its bind,
And His basic nature betray.

But God is not bound by time as are we,
Infinite – not bound by our ways;
God was there before time e'er began,
The Lord is the "Ancient of Days."

There'll be no time in Heaven, you know,
No calendar up on the wall;
No one will carry a watch on the wrist,
No grandfather clock in the hall.

Once we're released from the presence of time,
And go through eternity's door,
We'll be in God's presence – the Present Tense,
And time just will be no more.

Those who've gone to Heaven before,
And on through that great Pearly Gate,
Will not wonder why we are so slow,
In Heaven, you cannot be late.

Prayer: *Lord, with eagerness I anticipate an eternity with You – an existence without time, when all of life will be a constant NOW. The very thought stretches my mind.*

A LIGHT TO THE NATIONS

World wide missions is not just a New Testament idea. This concept is scattered throughout the Old Testament as well. One of those places is Isaiah 49, where Isaiah speaks as though he were the nation Israel. Verse 6 says it well – *"The Lord said to me, 'I have a greater task for you, my servant. Not only will you restore to greatness the people of Israel who have survived, but I will also make you a light to the nations so all the world will be saved.'"*

This was a time when the very survival of Israel was in question because of the oppression by Babylon. But Israel could think of nothing but survival—certainly not sharing its God with all the nations of the world.

The Lord did not get the world wide evangelism done back then because Israel was too self-centered. How sad that Israel could not fully grasp that God was not just a Jewish God! They had eyes only for themselves.

Ironic, isn't it, that the Lord now has the same struggle with the church? The self-centeredness and survival mind-set of so many churches today prevent them from being the power in world missions that God wants us to be.

A LIGHT TO THE NATIONS

God calls us to a greater task,
Just as with Israel of old;
But just like them, we'd rather bask
In glories of the past, retold.

"For all the world, you'll be a light."
Is what the Lord tells us today;
But in our selfishness, we fight
The call to show 'those folks' the way.

We pray, "Dear Lord, bless us today,
Bring back to us the strength of yore,"
While all this time He tries to say,
"Reach out – and you'll be strong once more."

Prayer: *Lord, help me to be a strong voice for missions in my church. And help my church to see that strength and growth come as we give ourselves to Your world wide outreach.*

WHAT ABOUT ME?

The introduction of Paul's first letter to Corinth includes some very unexpected statements. One is in verse 6: *"The message of Christ has become so firmly established in you that you have not failed to receive a single blessing.*

This is unexpected because the rest of the letter points out the many problems that were so prevalent in that church – areas where the message of Christ was not firmly established at all.

He goes on to say in verse 8: *"He will also keep you firm to the end so that you will be faultless in the Day of our Lord Jesus Christ."* How can these two ideas come to life in me? Is the message of Christ so firmly established in me that I do not fail to receive a single blessing? And what about being faultless?

WHAT ABOUT ME?

Is the gospel as firmly established in me
As in Corinth so long ago –
So that not a single blessing of God
I ever would fail to know?

I wonder how Paul could write them like that,
Then expose all their faults as he did;
It's hard to think of that church in this light,
Such sin – as Paul lifted the lid!

But what about me? Would he say it today?
Would Paul write the same about me –
That I am firmly established in God,
So all of His blessings, I'll see?

Prayer: *Lord, if You can make the church of Corinth faultless on the day of our Lord Jesus Christ, maybe there is still hope for me. I pray that You will do Your purifying work in me today.*

FAITH AND GOD'S WORD

The Apostle Paul's adventurous trip to Rome is recorded in Acts 27. As a part of that adventure, he experienced a ship-wreck in the Mediterranean Sea. The crew and passengers were in panic during the storm that destroyed their vessel. Finally they gave up all hope.

It was then that Paul took command, and in his "take-over" speech, he told of the word he had received from his God. Since none of the others aboard had heard from their gods, they all listened. His confidence and faith in God impressed them. What a great statement of faith he made in verse 25! *"So take courage men! For I trust in God, that it will be just as I was told."*

That is what faith means – that it will be just as I was told. It is explicit trust in the word of God. Not blind hope in an uncertainty or in an illogical dream. When God gives His word on something, I believe it. That is faith!

This means that the foundation of faith is knowing God's word, so we know what we can trust.

FAITH AND GOD'S WORD

Faith assumes I know what You say,
And that I know Your word;
That I'm alert from day to day,
So what You've said, I've heard.

By faith I know that it will be
Exactly as You said;
And what I've heard, some day I'll see,
Faith lets me see ahead.

So, help me be alert today,
To hear just what You say;
So that whatever comes my way,
Your word I shall obey.

Prayer: *Lord, I want to be a person of faith, and I realize that I can't be unless I hear and understand Your word. So, help me first of all, to be open and alert to Your word.*

TESTINGS AND TEMPTATIONS

How easy it is for us to confuse testing and temptation! They seem so similar because they both can be so unpleasant and even painful.

God tests us with the expectation of success and strength. This gives us the ability to endure and to become stronger. Testing is always a positive experience. Temptation is different, for God will not tempt anyone. The devil tempts us with the hope that we will fall and show our weakness. Temptation is always a negative experience.

James marks the difference for us in 1:12-13: *"Happy is the person who remains faithful under trials, because when he succeeds in passing such a test, he will receive his reward. ... If a person is tempted he must not say, 'This temptation comes from God,' for God cannot be tempted by evil and he himself tempts no one."*

Thank God for trials and testing because they indicate that the Lord expects us to succeed. They show that He has confidence in us.

TESTING AND TEMPTATIONS

Our trials come in many forms,
We welcome none at all;
Sometimes God tests to see our strength,
While hoping we won't fall.

The Bible says we're fortunate
When testings come our way,
For testings help us to endure,
Our strength then, to display.

Temptations, though, are different,
They come through our own lust,
The devil uses them to test
Us, and our will to bust.

God does not tempt us, but He gives
The power that we endure;
And when temptations we resist,
That helps us to mature.

Lord, I need wisdom straight from You,
To recognize Your test;
For when these trials are Your will,
I know You want the best.

Prayer: *Lord, I need wisdom to distinguish between Your testing, and the devil's temptations. I thank You that Your testing indicates that You expect me to succeed.*

GOD'S POWERFUL LOVE

One of the prominent aspects of God, that sets Him apart from all other deities, is His love for us. And this brings out a corresponding love in us.

Other of the world's deities instill fear in their followers, so that worship is not a love feast, but an experience of fear and placating the god. At the end of Romans 8, Paul gives us great insight into that marvelous love that God has for us. Verse 35 says it well: *"Who can separate us from the love of Christ? Can trouble do it, or hardship, or persecution, or hunger, or poverty, or danger, or death?"*

Then he states in verse 38 that nothing can separate us from the love of God:
- *neither death nor life,*
- *nor angels or other heavenly beings,*
- *nor the present or the future,*
- *or the world above or the world below.*

What a tremendous truth! Nothing can separate me from God's love – even me! There is nothing I can do, or that anyone else can do to stop God from loving me.

GOD'S POWERFUL LOVE

Not one thing in the universe
Could ever stop God's love;
There is no power that could coerce
Our father God above.

There is no power strong enough
To stop that love, I know;
There's nothing in the world so tough,
Such love, to overthrow.

To that great love, praise God, I'm bound,
Nothing can come between;
It is the greatest power around,
No one can intervene.

Not even anything I do
Could stop God's love for me;
With that tremendous thought in view,
From worry I'm set free.

Prayer: *Lord, I know I don't deserve it, but I praise You for Your love. It is constant, steady, and eternal. I thank You that there is nothing I can do to stop that great love. Lord, help me to reflect it to others today.*

LOVE, FAITH, AND HOPE

Because of the prominence we have given to 1 Corinthians 13, we always link faith, hope and love with the apostle Paul. But Peter wrote of these three virtues as well (in 1 Peter 1:21-22)

"... your faith and hope are fixed on God. Now that by your obedience to the truth, you have purified yourselves, and have come to have a sincere love of your fellow believers, love one another earnestly with all your heart."

Peter's message is very clear: faith and hope are fixed on God, while love is fixed on people. It is when we get these reversed that we get in trouble. We often try to love God without loving people, and we put faith and hope in people instead of in God.

Paul said these three qualities are lasting, but the greatest is love. How often have we taken that one statement out of context and tried to apply it to God! Even a casual reading of what Paul wrote in 1 Corinthians, tells us that he meant our love for other people.

Paul and Peter agree on this. Have faith in God, extend your love to people, put your hope in the Lord.

LOVE, FAITH, AND HOPE

We've missed the point Paul made of love,
And thought he wrote of God, above,
That faith and hope and love – all three
Were aimed at God in harmony.

But Peter wrote of these three too,
And gives to us a clearer view;
We fix on God, our faith and hope,
But Love's seen in a difference scope.

Our love is aimed at other folk,
Now isn't that how Jesus spoke?
"A new command I give to you,
To love the folks who are in view."

We often try to love the Lord,
While with a brother, in discord;
To love the Lord, there's just one way,
And that's to people – love display.

Prayer: *Lord, why have I mixed this all up? Help me find concrete ways to show love today to the people I meet, and to extend hope and faith to You.*

DO YOU LOVE ME?

So often we read the Bible carelessly, skimming it with our pre-conceived ideas in mind. An illustration of this is John 21:16-17, where Jesus questions Peter's love a week or so after the resurrection. Having breakfast with seven disciples who had fished in vain all night until He told them where to cast the net, Jesus asked Peter three questions about his love. It was not that He asked one question three times: they were three very different questions, all with the same answer.

> Q: **Do you love me more than these?**
> A: *You know that I like you.*
>
> Q: **Do you love me?**
> A: *You know that I like you.*
>
> Q: **Do you like me?**
> A: *You know that I like you.*

Why don't those who translate the Greek into English ever translate these questions correctly? The vast majority of translations just gloss over it as though it were unimportant. Peter could not use the same word for love that Jesus used; instead, he used the word for friendship. In fact, no one in the New Testament is recorded as telling Jesus, face to face: "I love You."

DO YOU LOVE ME?

Peter said, "Lord, I'm your friend,"
When asked if his love were real;
But note that he could not pretend
A love that he could not feel.

Something blocked his love that day,
Perhaps those words he had said:
"Though all the rest might turn away,
I'll be faithful 'til I'm dead."

Memory of that dreadful night,
When he said, "I don't know him!"
Filled his mind with dreadful fright,
He had yielded to a whim.

Now he met Jesus face to face,
With a chance to set things straight;
Still overcome by his disgrace,
That love he did frustrate.

He said, "I like You," that was all,
Of love, he could not speak;
In this trap, do I also fall?
Is my love for Him that weak?

Prayer: *Lord, I do want to tell You that I love You. But if Peter could not say it, can I? Search my heart to see if I really love You, or if I only like You.*

BLESSED, TO BE A BLESSING

Our praying is so often filled with cliches – such as, "Lord, bless us." Why are we so vague in prayer, not asking for anything more specific than a blessing? One of the first mentions of a blessing in the Bible is when God spoke to Abram in Genesis 12. The Lord spoke of a great and glorious new land He would give Abram, of his many descendants, who would become a great nation, and of the great family by which he would be known.

Maybe this is why we seek God's blessing – so we too can have fame, prosperity, and a great family. But the last part of verse 2 gives a different meaning to blessings. It gives insights into the reason and purpose that the Lord is eager to bless people. *"I will bless you and make your name famous so that you will be a blessing."*

"So that you will be a blessing" – that is the reason God is willing to bless me. But what if I want a blessing just for myself? Well, that's when blessings are cut off, for we are not the purpose of blessings, we are merely the channel through whom God's favor can be passed on to others.

BLESSED, TO BE A BLESSING

Now, why should God bless me today?
So often this is how I pray;
As in my praying day by day,
A selfish attitude betray.

But God has said within His word,
A truth more clear than just inferred;
His blessings are to be transferred,
Passed to another – then a third.

"I'll bless you," God has said to me,
So that you will then a blessing be."
To others' welfare, I'm the key,
There's purpose in God's gifts to me.

Prayer   *Lord, deliver me from the selfishness that prays for a blessing just for me. Instead, help me seek ways to be a blessing to others today. Let Your favor and mercy flow* **through** *me.*

THE IMPORTANCE OF OBEDIENCE

In the exciting story of Saul's conversion in Acts 9, we seldom give prominence to an obscure believer who quickly obeyed without much hesitation. Ananias of Damascus was not heard from before or after this event. But so much depended on his obedience.

Can you imagine the fear he must have had when in his vision God directed him to seek out the one man who was a threat to the safety of every believer in Damascus? It would have been so easy to continue his questioning and objecting, for he knew all about Saul of Tarsus and his mission to destroy this new movement of Messiah followers.

But one vision was enough, and Ananias was ready to contact the enemy with, *"Brother Saul, the Lord who appeared to you on the road has sent me..."*

One of the most amazing and refreshing things about these believers in Acts is their openness to new concepts, and willingness to step off into an uncertain future. Does that sound like churches today?

THE IMPORTANCE OF OBEDIENCE

Ananias knew from the start
That he also was on Saul's chart
Of those targeted for arrest,
And there was no use to protest.

For he knew Saul was on his way
To Damascus, to display
His hate and venom for all those
Whom he had chosen to oppose.

What a surprise when God appeared,
And so suddenly interfered,
Telling him to seek Saul out !
It's no wonder he had a doubt.

But he took the Lord at His word,
Acted on what he'd just heard,
Deciding right then to obey
Promptly, with no hint of delay

Is that the way I act today?
Is one time enough, to convey
That the Lord wants me to obey
In some most unexpected way?

Prayer: *Lord, I really want to be as obedient as Ananias was. Help me today to be alert to Your leading in my life.*

THE WHOLE ARMOR OF GOD

As a part of Paul's letter to the Ephesians, he gives good advice on how to protect oneself from the tricks and power of the Devil — *"Put on all the armor that God gives you."* (Ephesians 6:11)

We don't know if Paul underlined the word **all**, or if he emphasized it somehow, but that's where the emphasis belongs. If we neglect any one part of it, or try to depend on one part only, then we are in danger, This is the armor that God has provided - - - -

       Truth,

       Righteousness,

       Readiness to proclaim the gospel,

       Faith,

       Salvation,

       God's Word,

       Prayer.

All seven of these are for our defense against Satan's attacks. But the last two are also for offense, and with them we are able to attack the enemy. If any one of the seven is missing or weakened, we become vulnerable to defeat.

THE WHOLE ARMOR OF GOD

The Lord has given all we need
That from evil we would be freed;
God's given us a way to stand,
Protected from the Devil's hand.

The secret is to use it all,
So in defeat we will not fall;
He gives us truth and righteousness
To wear when we are in distress.

Our faith will shield us from attack,
But there's no armor for the back,
Which means we dare not turn around
When enemy attacks abound.

He also gives His word, and prayer,
Effective weapons anywhere,
So we can push the enemy
Out of our lives with victory.

But if we lack just one of these,
Then Satan will have all the ease
He needs to conquer and defeat,
Without them all – we can't compete

Prayer: *Lord, I thank You for equipping me so adequately for this battle. I want to use every piece of armor that You have given me.*

INTERCESSION

1 Chronicles 21 records King David's sin in taking a census of the nation. Actually it was more than a census; it was counting the men of military age – a reliance on military strength rather than on the Lord. David did this even though his commanding general advised against it.

After it was done, the Lord let him know it was a wrong thing to do, and sent a punishment on the nation. At that point we have a great example of what true intercession is. It is not just praying for someone else – but willingness to take another's punishment. 21:17 says it well:

"David prayed, 'O God, I am the one who did wrong, I am the one who ordered the census. What have these poor people done? Lord, my God, punish me and my family, and spare your people.'"

Intercession is stepping in between another and his punishment, willing to take another's punishment for him. We have watered it down to mean merely praying for someone.

INTERCESSION

We've weakened the word, 'intercede',

And we've made it mean only plead

For God to help someone in need,

That from his problems, he be freed.

It's willingness to step between

A friend and punishment foreseen;

It means that I will intervene

With: "Punish me – let him go clean."

Prayer: *Lord, I don't think I have ever really interceded for anyone this way – willing to take on myself someone else's punishment. Without that, my prayers for them seem so futile.*

FREE AT LAST!

The undergirding truth in Paul's letter to the churches in Galatia is centered on FREEDOM – freedom from the law and its restrictions. Whenever such an idea is emphasized, there are usually some who take that as a license to sin. But Paul puts them straight on the matter in 5:13-14 - - -

"As for you, my brothers, you were called to be free. But do not let freedom become an excuse for letting your physical desires control you. Instead, let love make you serve one another. For the whole Law is summed up in one commandment – Love your neighbor as you love yourself."

Our freedom in Christ is freedom to love our neighbors, because such freedom is the culmination of the Law. The Christ-like kind of freedom releases us to love, and gives us liberty from our sin, rather than permission to indulge our sin.

FREE AT LAST!

Freedom is a coveted thing,
Of its blessings we often sing,
Thinking that to us it will bring
   Ability to have our fling.

But it's not from the Law, I'm free
When Jesus came to rescue me –
Instead, it's freedom from my sin
When God's Spirit dwells within.

Freedom to love as ne'er before,
Freedom to open up the door
Of ministry to others' needs,
To live beyond the old stale creeds.

It's really not a "freedom from,"
But rather, freedom to become
All that the Lord wants me to be,
That's how Jesus makes me free!

Prayer: *Lord, I rejoice in the freedom that is a part of my salvation, but Lord, deliver me from the desires and inclination to distort that freedom by my own selfishness.*

GOD'S INTEGRITY TEST

In James 2:13 we see a basic principle of God's relationship with us: if we do not believe enough in a particular aspect of our relationship to others – enough to practice it ourselves, then God cannot grant it to us.

"For God will not show mercy when he judges the person who has not been merciful."

Jesus expressed the same principle when it came to forgiveness – *"If you forgive others the wrongs they have done to you, your Father in heaven will also forgive you. But if you do not forgive others, then your Father will not forgive the wrongs you have done."* (Matthew 6:14-15)

If I do not believe in mercy and forgiveness enough to extend it to others, then God will not give it to me. This is a very serious matter, and can be very disturbing.

GOD'S INTEGRITY TEST

Whene'er I ask God to forgive,
He takes note about how I live;
Have I really forgiven you
For those disturbing things you do?

And when it's mercy that I seek,
(For without it, life is so bleak.)
If I'm not merciful to you
Then I'll receive no mercy too.

The Bible says I can't receive
A thing in which I don't believe;
So first, I must look deep inside
To see what in me, might abide.

What I'm willing to give away
Determines what God will relay
On back to me, so I am blessed.
This is God's integrity test.

Prayer: *Lord, search my soul, and show me what You see. I do seek Your mercy and forgiveness, but now I know that unless I extend mercy and forgiveness to others, I cannot expect it from You.*

MY STEWARDSHIP OF WORDS

In James 3:6-12, James expresses a very negative and pessimistic evaluation of the tongue –

"The tongue is like a fire." (verse 6)

"It's a world of wrong, ... spreading evil through our whole being." (verse 6)

"It sets on fire the entire course of our existence with the fire that comes from hell itself." (verse 6)

"No one has ever been able to tame the tongue." (vs 8)

"It is evil and uncontrollable, full of deadly poison." (verse 8)

This sounds like something we would expect from *The Proverbs*, and indeed Solomon wrote many things that agree with James. We are stewards of the tongue and what we speak, how we speak. The human is the only one in God's creation who has been given the gift of speech, capable of great oratory, or simple encouragement, or fiery blasphemy.

How we control our speech is an integral part of our stewardship.

MY STEWARDSHIP OF WORDS

The product of my tongue and lip
Is a vital part of stewardship,
Because the words that I will say
Reveal what's inside me today.

You see – I am the only one
Who speaks for this phenomenon;
The words I use can hurt or heal,
And once they're said, there's no repeal:

I must manage my words so well
That no matter on whose ears they fell
I do not lead someone astray
By simply indulging in hearsay.

It's not only the obvious
Like words that hurt, or if I cuss,
That I must shun or throw away.
But I'm steward of each word I say.

Prayer: *Lord, my speech is the most difficult part of me that I must control, and I need Your help every day.*

Printed in the United States
26013LVS00003B/1-96